HAVING A BABY
CAN BE A SCREAM

Also by Joan Rivers

THE LIFE AND HARD TIMES OF HEIDI ABROMOWITZ
ENTER TALKING

HAVING A BABY CAN BE A SCREAM

Joan Rivers

W.H. ALLEN · LONDON
1987

Printed and bound in Great Britain by
Adlard & Son Ltd, The Garden City Press
for the Publishers W. H. Allen & Co. Plc
44 Hill Street, London W1X 8LB

British Library Cataloguing in Publication Data

Rivers, Joan
   Having a baby can be a scream.
   1. Pregnancy——Anecdotes, facetiae,
   satire, etc.   2. Childbirth——Anecdotes,
   facetiae, satire, etc.
   I. Title
   618.2'0207   RG525

   ISBN 0-491-03477-6

Contents

To Melissa
Without whom I wouldn't have needed this book

and

To Edgar
Without whom I wouldn't have had Melissa

LETTER FROM A REAL DOCTOR—

Joan Rivers is aptly named, for, like a river, she goes on and on...

Seriously, Joan - again like a river - has sparkle, vitality and depth. All these qualities are apparent in her book on a subject as old and broad as the Mississippi itself - Motherhood and Childcare.

Make no mistake. In between the inevitable gag lines, there are plenty of useful hints and sensible solutions to problems every young parent faces. Because Joan has almost total recall, she can trace her own experiences throughout prgnancy and her child's early years. Laugh along with her, but you will learn while you are laughing!

This book makes parenthood fun. It takes some of the fear and uncertainty out of situations that are brand-new and happening so quickly in the lives of its readers. Happily, its humorous viewpoint never interferes with its serious intent to help many young parents to relax and enjoy their children.

So, my advice to you is: Get out your goldrush pan and go prospecting. You'll find many golden nuggets of information in one of the fastest moving Rivers of them all -

Morrison S. Levbarg MD

11

Opening Monologue

WHEN my husband Edgar and I were courting, he said he couldn't wait to have a baby. It was only after we were married that he changed his mind and decided that I should have the baby. And that's when I got frightened.

Like most women, I had always wanted children, but when I finally got pregnant I was fraught with questions. Was I ready to become a mother? Did I know enough? And would the baby and I survive my amateur bumblings? Well, I was, I did, and we have.

And that's why I am writing this book. To let every pregnant woman (and man) out there know that you can smile your way in and out of the maternity ward. And all through motherhood, too. Well, almost.

Having a baby and becoming a mother should be a ball. Not a bawl. And yet throughout history women have passed down such tales of horror to each other ('I was in labour 108 days.' 'My doctor left more stitches in me than in an entire knitted dress.' 'They had to give me gas, plus an epidural, plus pethidine – and I still felt everything!') that almost every pregnant woman approaches the big event with fear and trepidation.

Some years ago I was almost one of them. I was scared silly. Mainly because my cousin Shirley, who never complains, screamed and screamed when she was having her baby. True, this was just during *conception*. But it put me off.

So, I started asking around exactly what was what. I rang and interviewed dozens of obstetricians, paediatricians and one chiropodist by mistake. I started asking them questions, questions, questions. Each one kindly gave me answers, answers, answers. (Except one obstetrician, who in order to avoid me moved to China and is now delivering babies by acupuncture.)

Mainly because of these conversations, and the knowledge that I acquired from them, when my Big Day came it was joyous and exciting – and well worth the minor pain and discomfort I

13

suffered when I broke two front teeth while biting down on a bullet.

Having a Baby Can Be a Scream is a summary of the dialogues that I had with many experts (who didn't always agree with each other) – and the chiropodist – but mostly it is the distillation of my exchanges with Dr Morrison Levbarg, a most distinguished Park Avenue paediatrician whose offices – and billing system – were always open and waiting for me.

And so, mama-to-be, sit down, prop this book on your tummy and read. This isn't meant to replace Dr Hugh Jolly. So keep him beside you. I hope these dialogues will also be a good bed companion in the absence of the real thing. So keep smiling. Remember, you never looked more radiant . . . from the neck UP.

JOAN RIVERS

CHAPTER I

Doctor, Why Are You Looking So Damn Cheerful?

I'LL never forget the first signs I had that made me think maybe I was pregnant. I found myself throwing up every morning, even when I wasn't thinking about Edgar's family, and I began to wake up in the middle of the night craving food instead of my husband. Finally I began to notice that I was having a harder and harder time seeing my toes, so I toddled off to my doctor. 'Doc,' I said to him, 'how do I know I'm pregnant?' He told me the first sign of pregnancy was a missed period. That didn't sound too bad. What he didn't tell me was that a baby nine months later was the second.

Of course, there are many other signs in between – such as enlargement and increasing sensitivity of the breasts and dizziness and nausea – but if you want to know fast, as I did, you can take a test as early as two weeks after you have missed your first period.

A word of caution should go in here. Pregnancy tests are not 100% reliable. If you take them too early they will give you a negative result even if you *are* pregnant. Take the case of my absent-minded friend Harriet. Harriet never could remember when she last had a period, and took her test when she was only one day overdue. Of course the result was negative, and it took Harriet another four months and five burst skirt zips to realize there might have been some mistake.

Anyhow, whether you take a pregnancy test or not, you should go and see your doctor as soon as you suspect you are pregnant.

Joan: How does one go about finding the best hospitals, and midwives, and obstetricians?

Doctor: Your women friends who are already mothers will clamour to solve this problem for you. Each woman always thinks *her* hospital/midwife is the best. The first qualification must be that they inspire confidence in you. Remember, your relationship with your doctor or midwife will help make this a safe and easy journey.

Joan: I've heard you get much more choice if you 'go private'. What is this safe and easy journey going to cost me if I decide to do that?

Doctor:	There is no set fee. Each doctor more or less has an average fee for his or her community, which most of his or her patients will pay. The best approach is an open one.
Joan:	With a pocketbook to match.
Doctor:	Come, come, Miss Rivers, surely you're not . . .
Joan:	Broke? My husband keeps saying we are. But that's impossible. I still have cheques left. That should help, don't you think?
Doctor:	Have a candid discussion with your doctor at the very beginning about fees. Remember, your doctor is a D★O★C★T★O★R and deserves a little respect. What does this white jacket tell you?
Joan:	That you moonlight as a Good Humour man?
Doctor:	Very few doctors today are wealthy. Why, just the high cost of living, keeping up a modern office – do you think Mies van der Rohe chairs come cheap? – not to mention bandages, aspirin and golf club membership.
Joan:	How often should I see my doctor?
Doctor:	During the first six months of your pregnancy, assuming all goes well, you should visit your doctor or midwife once a month. For the next two months, you might be asked to see him or her every two or three weeks. Some of these visits will be to the hospital. In the last month or so, weekly visits are the usual practice 'til the baby arrives.
Joan:	I guess I should be home when the kid arrives. It makes a better impression.
Doctor:	I would suggest a hospital.

Joan: Doc, I'm from a small town – Larchmont. The only hospital we have is Fred's Hospital & Grill and somehow I find it hard to trust a doctor whose sterilizer has hot dogs in it.

Doctor: You should check out the hospital carefully, especially to find out what their attitude is towards breastfeeding and natural childbirth. The hospital consultants or your own doctor can help here. They will book a hospital bed for you.

Joan: How will they know the date my baby's due?

Doctor: The doctors usually figure on 280 days from the first day of you last menstrual period. But no one knows exactly how long it will take your baby to develop. Be patient. Two weeks one way or the other should not be alarming.

Joan: Unless, of course, I'm in labour for those two weeks.

Doctor: You look like a nice, normal, healthy girl. I hardly think that will happen – not with proper care and exercise.

Joan: Exercise?!! Doctor, I'm Jewish. Jews don't exercise. We sell the equipment.

Doctor: Well, actually, strenuous exercises such as tennis, golf and riding are not especially recommended. Swimming is permissible if you avoid diving, violent surf and extremely cold water.

Joan: What would you recommend for me?

Doctor: Most doctors advise a healthy woman to walk every day even though she's doing housework. The important point is to stop before you're tired.

Joan: Oh, I never get tired of housework.

Doctor: Really?

Joan: I don't do any. When guests come to visit, I just put out dust sheets and say we're painting.

Doctor: Today we feel it is advisable for a woman to go on working while pregnant if she is in good health and if she wants to continue working. Most women maintain a healthier point of view during pregnancy if their way of life is not changed too sharply.

Joan: How long can a woman keep working?

Doctor: In fairly sedentary work, there's no reason why she can't continue working into her ninth month.

19

Joan: A friend of mine worked up until the end. She even had her baby right at work!

Doctor: What does she do?

Joan: She's a Delivery Room nurse.

Doctor: If she did work during her pregnancy, I hope she had a helping hand at home with the more strenuous housekeeping duties.

Joan: Oh, yes, her mother-in-law. She was always right there to help her throw out the empties.

Doctor: Anything more than a very occasional drink during pregnancy is unwise. And smoking ideally should be out for anybody pregnant. If you're a heavy smoker and can't give it up, at least you should cut down. The odd drink may have little effect on either the mother or her unborn child but it's best to cut out alcohol altogether – or at least to give up spirits. Drinking to the point of intoxication is bad on many counts. Being drunk makes a person more prone to accidental injury and drinks are high in 'empty calories', to name two.

Joan: And speaking of two, how about sex?

Doctor: Miss Rivers, I'm a married man!

Joan: Oh, not with you! I meant with Edgar – or someone who looks a lot like him – like Paul Newman.

Doctor: For a while it may have to be with no one. If a woman had had a history of miscarriage, most doctors would say the time when she would be having a period if she were not pregnant is an especially vulnerable one and that intercourse – as well as all other strenuous activities – should be eliminated then. However, there are many conflicting opinions. I personally believe that sexual activity is permissible as long as it is comfortable and pleasurable.

Joan: So that's what it's supposed to be like! What about sex towards the end of pregnancy?

Doctor: Some doctors recommend no sexual relationships during the last six weeks, but as they say, 'Love will find a way.'

Joan: 'They' say a lot of things, Doc, but it doesn't help. For example, whenever I'm worried they say, 'Relax, one day your ship will come in.'

Doctor: What's wrong with that?

Joan: I'm scared my ship will be the Titanic!

CHAPTER II

Not All Roads Lead To the Hospital

MOST of us by at least our eighth month of pregnancy know that it isn't Sir Stork or Pat Boone who will be delivering that little bundle from heaven the doctor has assured us is coming our way. And we know that we won't be tippy-toeing through the dewy garden one fine morning to find that bundle nestled under a cabbage leaf.

Oh, no. Television and the movies and Clare Rayner and Dear Marje have wised us up as to where babies come from.

But the route of delivery is something else . . .

Sometimes I hear women say, 'Oh I wouldn't be caught dead giving birth in a hospital.'

Kinda' mindless, when you stop to think of it. Like saying, 'I'd give my eyes to see the Taj Mahal.'

Still, if not in a hospital, where is the noble mother-to-be to divest herself of that treasure everybody says she had in her?

Doctor: Of course, you don't *have* to go to a hospital delivery room and deliver in the conventional manner. You have some other choices.

Joan: You mean, like the original earth-mother? Going into her hut and dropping the kid and being back out in the fields again twenty minutes later?

Doctor: Women do have some choice about how and where they will have their babies.

Joan: *How* they'll have their babies? Has the *British Medical Journal* come up with some new, improved way?

Doctor: Many women these days, in the first place, are opting for natural childbirth.

Joan: My idea of natural childbirth is going into labour wearing absolutely no makeup.

Doctor: Instead of natural childbirth you can think of it as being 'informed' or 'prepared' for childbirth.

Joan: If some I can think of were 'prepared', they wouldn't have to face childbirth at all.

Doctor: You've heard of Lamaze.

Joan: I've heard of Limoges.

Doctor: Well, this Frenchman Lamaze was the one who pioneered the techniques of natural childbirth. He considered drugs too expensive and too dangerous.

Joan: Oh, so he had visited Los Angeles.

Doctor: The Lamaze Method educates the pregnant woman on the birth process and how to relax uninvolved muscles. Husbands learn how to coach their wives during labour.

24

Joan: I can tell you I want no coaching from *my* husband. I expect him to be out shopping. I mean, really *shopping* for guess who.

Doctor: There are actually husband-coached childbirth classes where they show films and you see a child being born with the help of his or her father.

Joan: The kind of films I like is where they run the reels backward from childbirth to conception.

Doctor: Some women may like to consider a home birth. Just stop to think: most people who are over 60 years old today were born at home. Jimmy Carter, by the way, was the first American president to be born in a hospital.

Joan: Which certainly says something for home births.

Doctor: About half the babies born in Holland are born at home, and Holland has one of the lowest infant death rates of any developed country. The United States on the other hand, where hospital birth has come to be the rule, has one of the highest.

Joan: If you'd known some of the nurses I've known, you wouldn't wonder why. 'Could I have a bedpan, nurse?' 'Yeah, catch.'

Doctor: Home deliveries are only for women who are having a normal pregnancy. The key figure in a home delivery is likely to be a midwife. She'd normally be with you all through labour.

Joan: Even if I'm in labour 108 days?

Doctor: If labour is prolonged, a doctor will be called in.

Joan: But what if it's Wednesday when I'm finally going to pop? How will we know what golf course to find the doctor on?

25

Doctor:	One nice thing about home births is that you can have anybody there you want.
Joan:	Oh, great, why don't we stick up posters and sell tickets. 'Come and watch Joan putting (pushing) out.'
Doctor:	Now, now, Miss Rivers, don't be so cynical. You know, many women say that a home birth, in your own surroundings and with your family near at hand, can be a glorious, fulfilling experience.
Joan:	Glorious! Fulfilling! Doc, you've got to be joking. My family would be about as much use as a hole in the head. And as for Edgar's family . . .!
Doctor:	In some hospitals now there are birthing rooms with all the comforts of home. You labour and deliver right there.
Joan:	Just like home!
Doctor:	You might even find there's a bed big enough for your husband to lie alongside you during your labour.
Joan:	There's no bed big enough for that, believe me.
Doctor:	Well, you might prefer a birthing chair. Also, you can skip the enema, the shave, the drip. No hospital-issue gown – you wear what you want.
Joan:	Somebody get St Laurent on the phone and see if he can run me up something really smart for the birthing room.
Doctor:	Here I should say something about the Leboyer Method. Leboyer believed the emphasis should be upon what the baby sees, hears, and feels at the moment of entering the world. Everything should be done to reduce *his or her* trauma.

26

Joan: What about the mother's trauma?

Doctor: Lighting should be dim and indirect. There should be a minimum of noise and talking and hard, jerky movements. The newborn should be put into a tub of warm water with gentle, firm support to simulate the wet, weightless environment from which he or she just came.

Joan: You ought to be heavy with child and you wouldn't think it was a weightless environment.

Doctor: Anyway, the birthing room is ideally adapted for the Leboyer Method. Leboyer, you know, is the author of *Birth Without Violence*.

Joan: Didn't he also write *Fear Without Sex*?

Doctor: Really, Miss Rivers. As I was *trying* to say, an average hospital delivery is about four days but you can get sprung far sooner under an Early Discharge scheme.

Joan: Early discharge! I always thought that meant premature ejaculation.

CHAPTER III

Be Glad You're Pregnant

WHEN I found out I was pregnant, I was thrilled. It made me feel just like a teenager again. Also, my condition really proved most eloquently the fact that I was loved – if only for a moment. And best of all, it scotched those vicious lies about my age that the girls at the bridge club were spreading as it's impossible to be pregnant AND post-menopausal at the same time.

The only drawback was that as I got farther into my pregnancy, my clothes began to get tighter, and finally I had to put away even my roomiest garments and get some maternity clothes. The styles were charming, but who was I kidding? I knew that sooner or later, no matter what I put on, it would end up looking like a tent with a bow on top.

One terrific thing that happened was the way my breasts developed. It was probably the only time in my life that I could look into a mirror and ask, 'Mirror, Mirror, on the wall, who is the fairest of them all?' and not have the mirror answer, 'You are, Sir.' However, I didn't know about undergarments, and I remember asking my doctor . . .

29

WELCOME
TO THE
STORK CLUB

Joan: Are there such things as maternity bras? Do I need one? Remember, I'm a liberated woman. Well, half liberated. When my friends all burned their bras, I burned just one cup.

Doctor: Many women find they are more comfortable wearing a bra during pregnancy. But there's no need for any special type of support bra. As your breasts develop, a larger bra will become necessary. Remember, you will be gaining twenty or more pounds. That's why you need the support. As for tights, those blue ones you have on are a bit much.

Joan: I'm not wearing any tights.

Doctor: Well, if I were you, I'd slip into some support tights or elastic bandages to help you with those varicose veins. Also, it helps to lie down often during the day and use pillows to prop your legs up so they are higher than your hips.

Joan: What causes varicose veins?

Doctor: Poor circulation. Plus an inherited tendency to have them. Round garters and rolled stockings, which constrict the veins, can produce varicose veins in women who otherwise would not tend to have them.

Joan: I read that a woman shouldn't have a bath during the last six weeks of pregnancy. Is that true?

Doctor: No, it's not. In the old days doctors advised against baths, but nowadays we have found there is absolutely no harm in regular baths and showers. The only thing you should avoid during pregnancy is douching. However, bidets are safe, provided you have no vaginal bleeding.

Joan: So that's what a bidet is for! I always just put my feet in and play boats.

31

Doctor: Another thing you should do is see your dentist. During pregnancy your chances of getting cavities are greater. So NHS dental treatment is free during pregnancy and for a year after childbirth. You may use a local anaesthetic providing you've had no adverse reactions previously. Also, properly covered, you can have dental X-rays taken. But you should *always* tell your dentist if you are pregnant.

Joan: Great! I wanted to give Edgar a picture of me for Christmas, and the way I look now the only thing I'd dare give him is an X-ray.

Doctor: Now, now. Most women are at their most beautiful when they're pregnant. People will say, 'Look, she's glowing.'

Joan: It's from the heartburn! Another thing, Doctor – people keep saying I'm eating for two. Who are these two people? And why can't they do their own eating?

Doctor: That's just an expression meaning you are eating for yourself and the baby. But it doesn't mean you can gorge yourself. You must eat a balanced healthy diet, and watch your figure during pregnancy.

Joan: During pregnancy. I'll be the only one who *will* be watching my figure.

Doctor: You should not gain more than 20 pounds while you're pregnant, as too much weight may cause complications. Also, it's hard to lose the weight afterwards. But if a woman is careful about what she eats, she won't have this problem.

Joan: In other words, if it tastes good, spit it out.

Doctor: Eat a well-balanced diet with sufficient bulk from leafy vegetables to help with natural elimination. A good portion of meat, fish or eggs every day. Liver at least once a week. Grain products – preferably whole-grain breads and cereals. And, of course, a multivitamin supplement with minerals and iron which the doctor will prescribe.

Joan: Ha! Doctor, I caught you. You forgot the most important thing: milk! Every day she must drink milk!

Doctor: A woman doesn't have to drink milk if it's objectionable to her. She can consume it in other ways, such as in cream soups, custards, creamed vegetables. However, milk is rightfully called the most perfect food and contains the minerals needed for baby's bones and teeth, as well as being rich in so many other nutrients.

Joan: In general, I gather I should go heavy on the protein: meat, eggs, seafood, cheese, milk. A pregnant woman needs 50% more protein than she normally would. Correct, Doc?

Doctor:	Right. How come you're so clever?
Joan:	'Cause I'm writing this book. And the least I can do is keep one step ahead of you.
Doctor:	So then you know about all the foods you shouldn't be eating. All the fatso things and sugars and starches. Fat meats, rich puddings, sweets, soft drinks, gravies, bacon, pies, cakes, spaghetti, macaroni – though small amounts of wholemeal pasta are OK.
Joan:	There just went my breakfasts. Now what do I give up for lunch and dinner?
Doctor:	Miss Rivers, if you were really thin I would tell you this is the perfect time to gain weight. There is no definite relationship between weight gained in pregnancy and the size of your child. So no need to worry that gaining too much weight will make the baby larger and delivery more difficult. The largest portion of the baby is the head, which has no fat deposits.
Joan:	Then how come the world is so full of fatheads?
Doctor:	Miss Rivers, that joke makes me ill!
Joan:	Maybe it's morning sickness. I have a great cure for it: don't get up 'til afternoon.
Doctor:	There are ways to avoid morning sickness. Try eating something before you get up.
Joan:	How can you eat while you're asleep?
Doctor:	I mean before you get out of bed. Something bland, dry and a bit filling. Like water biscuits or meiba toast. Then stay in bed for another half hour. Also, to avoid nausea during the day, don't let your stomach feel empty. Keep things handy to nibble on, such as cheese, dried fruits and nuts.

Joan:	How long does morning sickness go on? Into the middle of the night?
Doctor:	It's usually over by the end of two and a half to three months.
Joan:	What about medicines? Can I keep taking the pills I used to take?
Doctor:	What pills did you take?
Joan:	Birth control pills.
Doctor:	No. Be particularly careful to use only those drugs your doctor approves for you. Then there's no chance that the developing embryo can be harmed.
Joan:	Yes, but what about me? Will pregnancy leave me a marked woman for life?
Doctor:	You mean the stretch marks that may appear during the last months of pregnancy? The answer is no. After the baby, they will gradually become smaller and thinner and eventually they will become only faint silvery streaks.
Joan:	What can I do to prevent them?
Doctor:	Nothing, really. Whether such streaks appear and how streaked your skin becomes depends in part on how much your stomach expands because of the size of your baby and how much excess fat you acquire. These marks can be minimized by avoiding any rapid gains. You can try massaging your tummy with lanolin or cold cream daily during the last four months to ease the stretched condition of your skin.

Joan: Pregnancy is sure a fun time for a woman. I've heard that another thrilling experience a lot of us can look forward to is acne.

Doctor: The acne, when it occurs, is temporary and no special treatment is required, though some doctors recommend a particular soap. Anyway, I wouldn't worry about acne, unless you had it when you were an adolescent. Did you have a skin problem as a teenager?

Joan: Did I! I had such a skin condition that for two and a half years I was quarantined for chicken pox. Which is one of the reasons I can't wait to buy my 'mask of pregnancy.' Where do I get it and will I be able to use any of my credit cards?

Doctor: The mask of pregnancy refers to a brownish discolouration which may appear on the face during pregnancy, but which fades gradually after delivery, like a suntan.

Joan: What about freckles? Are they also due to poor nutrition?

Doctor: No. During pregnancy your skin takes up brown pigments more rapidly. Either from exposure to the sun or wherever there has been any inflammation or scar tissue formation.

Joan: Well, now, let me tick off all my glamorous features. I'll have silvery streaks, varicose veins, a mask and freckles. Oh, and I've heard my glorious halo of hair will become dry and break off.

Doctor: Don't worry about hair breaking off and getting dry. After the baby is born, it will return to normal. But meanwhile, brush your hair regularly and massage your scalp.

36

Joan: Doc, there must be some other really kicky, giggly things that could happen to me. Tell me, tell me, tell me. . . .

Doctor: Well, you could break out in rashes because of your tendency to perspire. So bathe and powder those surfaces that are likely to become moist.

Joan: Does that include my mouth?

Doctor: Also, headaches may occur during the first three months of pregnancy. Especially among women who suffer pre-menstrual headaches. Just treat them as you would ordinary headaches.

Joan: I usually treat a headache by taking two aspirins.

Doctor: That's fine.

Joan: . . . which I rub on my forehead.

Doctor: Well, *that*'s OK. You should avoid paracetamol during early pregnancy, though it is safe in later months. Avoid aspirin in the later months. Headaches aside, during the last weeks of pregnancy your sleep may be disturbed for a number of reasons. The strong activity of your baby and the pressure of the enlarged abdomen make it difficult for you to find a position which is comfortable for any length of time. Try hot milk. Or the classic ploy of counting sheep. Take a sleeping pill *only* with your obstetrician's or doctor's permission.

Joan: When will the baby become a pain in the neck, or should I say, the stomach?

Doctor: During the last weeks. When the baby is growing large and heavy and the abdominal cavity feels crowded. But pain may also be felt over the bladder region – where the head of the baby is likely to press – or in the hip or the groin or along the margin of the lowest rib on either the right or left side. But none of these pains is really significant. All of them can be alleviated with paracetamol; aspirin is best avoided in the last month of pregnancy.

Joan: Come on, Doc. Sometimes I really wonder if the baby is worth all this. Pains – and more pains – and looking ugly are all you can promise me.

Doctor: Ah, but all your sufferings will be worthwhile once the patter of little feet is heard about the house.

Joan: I already hear the patter of little feet. I have a miniature dachshund.

Doctor: I'm sure your husband can cheer you up. Let him help you with household chores and let him take you out to dinner often.

Joan: Are you kidding? Yesterday I said, 'Edgar, I'd like to eat out.' He kicked my plate onto the fire escape.

Doctor: Miss Rivers, a husband should be involved with the pregnancy. Isn't your husband pleased you're pregnant?

Joan: I'm not so sure. When I telephoned to tell him the great news, he told me to hold on.

Doctor: Isn't he excited about the big event?

Joan: The only big event to him is the football results.

Doctor: Well, you must involve your husband. For example, let him purchase the basic wardrobe which should consist of four vests, nappies, four nightgowns, three baby stretch suits and two shawls.

Joan: Great, but what will the baby need?

Doctor: That's exactly what the baby will need. Along with a room of his own – if possible.

Joan: Why should the kid be lucky enough to have a room of his own when I still have to share mine with my husband?

Doctor: It will help him build better sleeping habits.

Joan: I've told my husband the same thing. That climbing onto the top bunk every night is getting to be a drag.

Doctor: The baby's room should be quiet, well ventilated and easily heated. It is important that the humidity be kept at a proper level so the baby's nose and mouth membranes won't dry out. Some people use a cradle or carry-cot at first, but get a cot for the baby within six weeks or two months. Get one with a side that can be raised or lowered and with a firm mattress (covered with waterproof material) that can also be raised or lowered. The mattress should be at hip level during the first few months, so you don't have to stoop to lift the baby.

Joan: What else is needed?

Doctor: About four or six sheets – the fitted kind. And remember: the baby's sheets should be changed each time they are soiled and at the very least three times a week. Also, make sure you have four cotton blankets and two heavier ones. If you decide on a cot duvet rather than blankets, have at least two covers, and wash the duvet itself every time it gets wet or soiled. Cleanliness is a must for a baby.

Joan: Thank God, they soon grow out of it. What else should be in the baby's room?

Doctor: A wardrobe or chest to keep his or her clothes in. A comfortable chair for you and a steady table next to it to hold the feeding paraphernalia. Also, you'll need something with a hip level surface to change and dress the baby on. The top of a low chest of drawers will do — if it's well padded and has raised sides so the baby can't fall off.

Joan: I know just what you mean. We could have done with raised sides to our bed on our wedding night. Was *that* a disaster.

Doctor: Miss Rivers, *please*, I really don't want to know . . .

Joan: Some men smoke after making love – Edgar smoked during. And he had the nerve to ask me for a light. I said, 'Get it yourself from the dashboard and don't disturb the bus driver.'

SEYMOUR XAVIER SCHAINHOLZ, M.D.

Dearest Joanie,

I assume by the time you get this, you and little Melissa will be well
ensconced and happy at home.

You were such a good patient and you gave me so many good laughs, I
almost hate to bring up the delicate matter of remuneration. But to
paraphrase an old saying, "Doctor, cannot live by laughs alone"--(unless
those laughs will keep you in stitches. Ha, ha).

I am sure a celebrity of your stature is accustomed to being "comped"
much of the time in restaurants and hotels and night clubs and the like
and something you said here one day gave me the impression you had
the impression your baby would also be "on the house."

However, as you know, a great deal of my practice is made up of cele-
brities and I ask you to consider where I'd be if I started "comping" my
patients.

Anyhow, I'm sorry to have to bring the matter up at all and please be
understanding about the embarrassing necessity of presenting you with
a bill.

Your most humble and grateful physician,

42

CHAPTER IV

Just Because
You're Lying Down,
Doesn't Mean
You're Lying In

*N*o woman really likes to go to a hospital unless she's having a fling with some doctor. But if one must do 'time' at a hospital, it's nice to come back with a little bundle. Especially if that little bundle is filled with a baby.

To help prepare myself for the blessed event, I exercised all through pregnancy, even though it looked silly. Did you ever see a bunch of pregnant women running round a gym? We looked like a netball game where every player had the ball.

I also took a natural childbirth course. It was terrific. They used to put all of us pregnant women into tracksuits and lay us down on the floor to do our exercises. We looked like a relief map of the Rocky Mountains. They explained everything that would happen during labour. At the end, they even showed a film of a woman giving birth to her baby. I enjoyed that part the most. But for some reason, they threw me out of the class. Maybe it was because I asked them to run the film backwards. 'Come on, nurse,' I shouted, 'now let's see the baby disappear.'

However, when the time came, I didn't have natural childbirth. I had a Jewish Delivery. They knocked me out when I
had the first pain and woke me up when my hairdresser, Mr
Phyllis, got there.

And was I glad he came. I had no brush or comb with me. I
had been so nervous when I was packing my bag. You see, I
didn't listen when my doctor told me at the start of the ninth
month, 'It's good to pack your bag and have it ready – just in
case.'

The girls I grew up with all seemed to have their bags packed
in their fifth month. I can remember the Larchmont paper was
always carrying an item that started out, 'Born prematurely to
Mr and Mrs Dick Bizzy was a 14-pound baby boy.'

Of course, I still have a bag I packed when I was single. I used
to call it my Survival Kit. . . .

Doctor: Your suitcase for the hospital should have several
fresh nightdresses, cosmetics and toiletries, a
dressing gown and slippers, a sanitary belt and
nursing bras.

Joan: My weekend Survival Kit had the same things in it!
Say, how much notice does a woman get that she's
going to have a baby?

Doctor: Nine months if she's married. Five months if she
isn't.

Joan: No, no, I mean at the start of labour.

Doctor: On average, 12 to 24 hours for the first baby. Fewer
for succeeding ones. Your doctor or midwife will
describe the signs and symptoms of labour and how
and when to ring the midwife or hospital. The
important thing is not to eat any heavy meals once
labour begins and drink only clear liquids.

46

Joan: Like vodka and gin?

Doctor: As *un*like them as possible. It's a good idea to go off booze altogether.

Joan: Can the baby do anything to hurry up the birth?

Doctor: No. The baby is just a passenger. Or an 'easy rider' if you will.

Joan: What happens when I get to the hospital?

Doctor: Well, when you arrive at the hospital and you're in labour –

Joan: I know, I know. I get booked in as two people.

Doctor: No, you'll be examined by the midwife and admitted to the labour ward where you will be looked after by a midwife throughout labour.

Joan: Not me. I don't get along with midwives. They're vicious to women. When my friend Trudie was in labour, the midwife looked down at her and said, 'Still think blondes have more fun?'

Doctor: I don't think that's true of most midwives.

Joan: Junior doctors scare me even more.

Doctor: How can that be? Junior doctors are full-fledged doctors. They are completely qualified.

Joan: They're too young. How can you have confidence in a doctor who has his rubber gloves pinned to his sleeves? My sister had a doctor so young, when he bent over to examine her, a tube of Smarties fell out of his pocket. She found it hard to trust in him, especially when they got into the delivery room.

Doctor: Why?

Joan: He saw the bars on the windows and began to shout, 'How will the stork get in?'

Doctor: I'll grant you delivery rooms aren't the comfiest-looking places in the world. They'll put you on the delivery table if you're going to have a normal delivery. If you're having a caesarian delivery they'll probably move you to another room for your operation.

Joan: Where will my husband be while I'm giving birth in the delivery room?

Doctor: If it's normal delivery he is encouraged to be there, giving you help, and support. If it's a caesarian he will probably be asked to wait outside the room. He'll get to see mother and baby pretty soon, though.

Joan: Doctor, here is what I am trying to say. It's not that I don't trust my husband. (Ha-ha-ha.) But I had a friend, Muriel. While she was in labour, her husband Manny was getting tipsy with a nurse, and as a joke, they short-sheeted her bed.

Doctor: Miss Rivers, don't you trust your husband?

Joan: I used to. Then as a joke I got into a taxi and said to the driver, 'Where can a girl get a little action in this town?' He took me to Edgar's office!

CHAPTER V

Coming Home to a Brave New World

I will never forget the day I came home from the hospital. Even though I had only been gone a week, the flat looked great – just the way I had left it – filthy. For all during pregnancy I hadn't bothered to clean. I felt that why should I bother to clean a rug that I couldn't see when I looked down?

I must admit when I first saw my kid she was no beauty. I had been told that most children were not much to look at at birth, but I really wasn't prepared for what I got. Her eyes were closed, her legs were bowed and her hair was wet and matted. I couldn't believe it – she looked just like Edgar's side of the family. By the time we left the hospital, however, she was adorable, which is a good thing because if she hadn't been – as I told my doctor . . .

Joan:	I would have switched kids.
Doctor:	No way. They have a very strict system today to make certain the mothers go home with their own babies. They put an identification bracelet on the baby as soon as it's born. I guess you could say, 'To each her own.'
Joan:	How long after the baby is born can I get up?
Doctor:	The sooner the better. Usually within 12 hours after the great happening.
Joan:	Just like on my honeymoon!
Doctor:	The longer a person stays in bed, the weaker she feels on getting up. Walking is good for circulation. Today doctors get women up fast and let them leave the hospital usually after two to three days.
Joan:	Great, without my husband, what fun can the hospital be – if you get what I mean (wink-wink-wink).
Doctor:	I think I do.
Joan:	In plain language, how soon can sexual activity be resumed after having a baby?
Doctor:	Well . . .
Joan:	I guess it's best to wait for a few days?
Doctor:	As soon as you want, but for some women it can take several weeks for the body to heal and adjust.
Joan:	After I have my baby, will I ever get my old figure back?
Doctor:	With proper exercise, of course you will.
Joan:	Damn it! My old figure was lousy. I want a new one.
Doctor:	Your husband told me the same thing.

Joan: Now that I am to become a mother – and I hope I'll always be able to live up to the exciting challenge of that role – my thoughts turn to circumcision. Are you for it?

Doctor: Only for boy babies. And only then if the doctor advises it. Circumcision is not done as a routine today.

Joan: I get depressed just thinking about them having to cut my poor little baby.

Doctor: Some women have periods of depression after giving birth. But the mood will usually pass in time. These depressions have a physical rather than psychological origin. During pregnancy the system of the mother is flooded with hormones which disappear right after the baby's birth.

Joan: Very often along with the baby's father! Now I am depressed and panicked about taking care of my baby at home. How will I know when it's hungry or whether it's too warm or cold?

Doctor: Babies are tough. They don't break. Think of all the mothers down through history who have given birth without the benefit of doctors or the benefit of hospitals.

Joan: Or the benefit of clergy! Anyhow, I'm scared to be alone with the kid. I mean, we hardly know each other.

Doctor: Being alone with your baby is not a frightening experience. All you need is a little common sense, concern for the baby's welfare, and lots of love. All your baby will want for the first few months is to be warm, full and dry.

Joan: Big deal! That's all I want!

Doctor: You'll be able to cope with your baby, I assure you. If you can get a helping hand from someone the first few weeks your baby is at home, that's all to the good. But make sure that hand is peeling the potatoes and dusting the furniture instead of handling the baby. That's your job.

Joan: But how about someone that could do both?

Doctor: Fine, if she's a mother's help who likes to do housework. But that's not a very probable combination.

Joan: You have to watch out for some of these mother's helps. They sometimes get confused about who they're supposed to be helping. A friend of mine caught her husband with their mother's help. He claimed she was just showing him how to burp their baby. My friend was furious. She told her husband, 'Get off her shoulder.'

Doctor: Maybe your friend's husband was starved of affection. Often the husband feels left out. Even though he may be very interested in the new addition to the family, it may be that a glance a day can very well satisfy his curiosity. Remember, you and the child have been keeping company all these months. Daddy may be frightened by something so tiny and fragile.

Joan: That was his excuse on our wedding night.

Doctor: It could have been yours, too. I beg your husband's pardon, Miss Rivers. Was your wedding night a dud?

Joan: Was it! It was such a dud we postponed the marriage for four weeks. But it was mostly my fault. On my wedding night I should have known better than to wear a nightgown with feet.

Doctor: I hope you're a little more adroit in knowing how to dress the baby. Because your husband is going to learn by watching you.

IF YOUR CHILD HAS A TENDENCY TO THROW UP AFTER MEALS, ALWAYS SEAT HIM NEXT TO PEOPLE YOU HATE

Joan: If that's the case, the kid is in double trouble. I can't see my husband changing a nappy that has anything in it. And if it doesn't have anything in it, why change it?

Doctor: It is true that if nappy-changing were the test of a father's love, probably most dads would be found wanting in fatherly love. Now's the time when you've got to get your husband in the habit of sharing the workload. The best suggestion I have is that when you're ready to leave the hospital, you plan the trip home so that you, your husband and the baby are alone together. It may be the first time.

Joan: The way things happen these days it may also be the last.

Doctor: Even when you are breast-feeding, your husband can encourage and support you. *And* he can give the baby expressed milk in bottles.

Joan: Do you believe in breast-feeding?

Doctor: I do, indeed. But only for babies.

Joan: I read somewhere that breast milk is for babies and cow's milk for calves. What's the difference, besides the containers they come in?

Doctor: Although mother's milk is ideal, there are some excellent babymilk formulas available today. They have been modified so that they are as similar as possible to breast milk. Straight cow's milk is not suitable for small babies, but a good babymilk formula is perfectly all right.

Joan: Then the bottle's as good as the breast?

Doctor: No! There are still many pluses in breast-feeding. Chief among these are fewer digestive upsets for baby. Less sicking up. Less diarrhoea. And no constipation. And perhaps a feeling of closeness that's hard to find in a bottle.

Joan: Try explaining that to a bankrupt dairy farmer's wife.

Doctor: Well, allergies seldom develop as they sometimes do with cow's milk. Also, a breast-fed baby has fewer skin rashes and greater immunity to infection.

Joan: It also gets used to crowds earlier – if the mother decides to breast-feed in public!

Doctor: Breast-feeding is great for the mother. It helps the organs involved in birth return to normal very quickly. And it's a great way for you and your baby to get to know each other!

Joan: What if a mother decides she doesn't want to breast-feed?

Doctor: As I said, there are excellent babymilk formulas that are perfectly nutritious and safe. While you're giving your baby a bottle you can also give him all the loving, cuddling and fondling he needs for his emotional security. And there should be no guilt. Not all mothers were meant to breast-feed.

Joan: What if you're all revved up for breast-feeding and the baby doesn't want to feed?

Doctor: Don't be dismayed if this happens at first. In any case you will not produce breast *milk* for the first three or four days but a thickish yellow milk-like substance called colostrum. New-born babies need frequent short feeds for the first four days. When the breast milk comes in feeds will be longer.

Joan: Do babies automatically take to breast-feeding? I'd hate to have the baby reject me the minute it sees my breasts. It would bring back such awful memories of adolescence.

Doctor: Babies sometimes need some directing. You can help
by holding the baby so his mouth can reach your
nipple and by helping him to take the brown circle
behind the nipple in his mouth, as well as the nipple.
This will keep the nipples from becoming sore. Be
sure to hold your breast away from your baby's nose
so he can breathe easily.

Joan: I guess that's where the expression 'Smother Love'
came from.

Doctor: There are other manifestations of 'smother love',
which we can go into later.

Joan: Is breast-feeding idiot-proof? I mean, is it possible to
flunk the course?

Doctor: Occasionally a mother does fail, even after she's
followed all the directions. But she hasn't failed her
baby, and she shouldn't blame herself. Attitude has
a great deal to do with success in breast-feeding.
Most mothers can breast-feed successfully if they are
determined, keep trying and have lots of
encouragement.

Joan: I don't know, Doc. How smart is a newborn kid,
really? I think I'll keep my kid on bottles. He won't
know the difference. I'll just take his bottle and
shove it into my bra. I'm afraid with all that nursing I
might become 'The Sensuous Mother of the Year.'

Doctor: Yes. Breast-feeding is very pleasurable to both
mother and child, even though it may hurt at first to
have the baby tugging at your nipples. But they
toughen up soon enough.

Joan: How long should the baby feed?

Doctor: Probably at least ten minutes on each breast per
feed, longer if the baby wants. Only restrict feeding
time if your nipples are sore, particularly in the early
days.

Joan: Should he alternate faucets, so to speak?

Doctor: Sometimes a baby will take both breasts at one feed, other times only one side. You should make sure the baby feeds on both sides during the course of the day. Remember to keep your nipples clean and to wash your hands before you touch them.

Joan: What position should I take when breast-feeding – besides hiding in the cupboard.

Doctor: There is nothing to be ashamed of. Breast-feeding is a wonderful and natural thing. So come out of the cupboard and choose whatever position is most comfortable and relaxing for you. Sitting in a rocking chair listening to the radio is very popular.

Joan: Yes. But some positions are bad for the mother. A friend of mine, a Yoga disciple, liked to nurse while standing on her head. It was great for the baby, but she was rather well endowed and ended up with two black eyes.

Doctor: That joke certainly wraps it up for today. Make sure the nurse sees you on the way out.

Joan: Why?

Doctor: She can always use a good laugh.

CHAPTER VI

Out of Those Girdles – and over the Hurdles!

*T*HE minute I had Melissa, Edgar started to complain. 'Why can't you look like you looked on the day we got married?' he would rant. 'Because I'm no longer pregnant,' I'd yell back. But he was right. After the baby you should do some exercises to get back into shape.

Once Melissa was born I got busy right away with exercising. The most delightful 'after-birth' exercise I found was opening presents, but the easiest was just to lie on my back and contract and relax my tummy muscles in and out.

Once I got home my doctor told me when I could begin strenuous exercises such as this one for the tummy. Lie down on the floor, raise your legs together until they're straight up, then slowly lower them to the floor to the count of 10. If you like, put on a record or the radio to keep you company.

Many women like to do the exercises on TV, others prefer the floor. Either way is okay. Just remember, the only way you can get back to your old shape is by hard work. Avoid all those masseurs who promise to take five pounds off you at each visit. The five pounds you'll lose will be from your purse.

For the new mother, like everyone else, walking is the best all-round exercise. I really made it into a fun activity, as each day I set a goal for myself – like Tiffany's or Cartier's.

My doctor told me when I was able to rejoin my gym class that weight-lifting can be great for bust rehabilitation. But take care. Avoid the mishap of one poor absent-minded woman in my class who was trying to get her bust back in a hurry. By mistake she picked up two weights and worked out with them vigorously, completely unaware that one of them weighed five pounds and the other ten. Since then she's been known as 'the odd couple'.

CHAPTER VII

It's A Boy
It's A Girl . . .
It's an Animal

*T*HE The first thing that really drove me crazy about Melissa was the amount of food she could put away. And what drove me even crazier was that it went in one end and immediately out the other. Things went through her so fast that I figured the wisest thing I could do was to feed her on the potty.

But, I let her enjoy herself. After all, I figured she was taking after my side of the family. I have a cousin Shirley who eats like the Martians have just landed at Dover. She once stayed the night at my house. The next day I couldn't believe the amount of food she put away – 4 pizzas, 10 pints of milk, 2 loaves of bread, 2 fried chickens and a large block of neapolitan ice cream. And that was just for breakfast!

Watching Melissa eat gave me a lot of pleasure for two reasons. One, I figured she really was enjoying herself, and two, she was still too young to realize what a terrible cook I am. Bad cooking runs in my family but who cares? We've all survived. My mother, for example, was a terrible cook. For the first ten years of my life I was brought up on radio dinners. Then she switched to TV dinners. Mother would stand over us and insist we eat them, and boy they tasted horrible – as she never warmed them up.

However, again, because I knew what was going to happen, I wasn't worried. I remember asking my doctor . . .

Joan: How many times a day should a child eat?

Doctor: Every child is different. Some like to eat eight times a day. Others might just give you a break and let you off with five meals. Today, most doctors let the child set the timetable. It's known as 'self-demand' schedule.

Joan: What does that mean? That my kid won't have regular meal times?

Doctor: Relax, relax, Miss Rivers. No child should be force-fed. Stuffing a baby is no way to demonstrate love. A child should eat when it wants to. Adults jump the gun on mealtimes if they're hungry. Haven't you been hungry and grabbed a snack when you really shouldn't have?

Joan: Yes. On my wedding night. A lot of couples eat hors d'oeuvres after they've made love. I ate mine instead.

Doctor: I'll bet your husband was upset.

Joan: I'll say. I ate all the filled ones.

Doctor: Try to feed your baby in a nice, quiet atmosphere and try not to have any interruptions. That way you'll make a friend of the baby, and he'll think the world's a friendly place.

Joan:	And what an idiot he'll grow up to be!
Doctor:	I hate to detect this note of cynicism in you, Miss Rivers.
Joan:	It's not a note, it's a scale. I was born and raised in New York where not too many people are friendly. Taxi drivers go right past you and give you the peace sign. Or half of it.
Doctor:	Well, the world can be a warm and friendly place for babies if we just try to take care of their needs sensibly and with love. For example, they eat for two reasons. One, because they are hungry, of course. Two, because they love to suck. So give them a long enough time at each feeding to enjoy themselves or they will take cravings out on something else. Like a thumb. And remember, stop several times during each feed for a burp.

Joan: What if I don't want to burp?

Doctor: Not you, you idiot. The baby. Remember to burp the baby. This will help prevent indigestion or colic. Also, if the baby's crying an hour or so after his last feeding, chances are he has a little indigestion, so pick him up and burp him, or try giving him a couple of ounces of water.

Joan: How about some milk mixed with soda water?

Doctor: No way, but you might try a dummy. They help satisfy the baby's need for sucking.

Joan: Doctor, somewhere I read that most babies require a 2 a.m. feed. This upsets me as that's usually the hour I'm coming in and I don't like to get milk on my spangles.

Doctor: Cheer up. If that baby is halfway reasonable, somewhere between his third and seventh week he should be snoozing through until 3 or 3.30 a.m.

Joan: Great! That's when my husband gets in. And he doesn't mind getting milk on his spangles, but he might object to getting something else on them.

Doctor: I presume, Miss Rivers, you are referring to the baby's bowel movements. Just don't be dismayed if there are no BMs the first day.

Joan: Dismayed! I'll be dismayed when they start coming!

Doctor: If the baby is breast-feeding, you can expect several movements a day, maybe one after each nursing.

Joan: Doctor, you have just made the most eloquent argument for bottle-feeding I ever heard.

Doctor: The bottle-fed baby usually has between one and four movements a day. The movements should decrease after the first month or so.

Joan: This morning on the radio I heard a golden oldie: 'Every Little Movement Has a Meaning'. Do you suppose some baby inspired that song?

Doctor: As far as your baby is concerned, every little movement means things are okay. Don't get uptight about any changes in colour or frequency. But, if the consistency of the stool changes drastically, you should tell the doctor.

Joan: In other words, I'll have to be a stool pigeon for my own kid!

Doctor: Absolutely. Watch the stool carefully and also how your baby is passing it. Frequency of movements is no gauge to constipation. A baby is constipated when his stool is so hard he can't pass it without straining, or when it comes out in little balls.

Joan: How does one treat constipation in a baby?

Doctor: No laxatives and enemas unless prescribed by your doctor. A little more water or sweetening in the milk-feed should loosen up the situation.

Joan: Then there's the other end of the rainbow . . .

Doctor: Diarrhoea? Cut down on the sweetening in the formula. If it persists, you should take the child to the doctor at once. Meanwhile, a sachet of Dioralyte – obtainable from a chemist – and boiled water might usefully be administered.

Joan: This whole discussion, as I see it, points in only one direction. Toward a pile of nappies about as high as Mount Everest.

Doctor: I must say, you're a woman of remarkable perspicacity.

Joan: Only when it's warm outside and I've been very active.

Doctor: The point is, until baby is trained you are going to have to change a lot of nappies unless you want a nappy rash on your hands –

Joan: On my hands! My God, I can get a rash just by touching the nappy? Now I'm ready to believe you really can get syphilis off a toilet seat.

Doctor: If you want to keep the baby from getting a nappy rash, you had better change him or her before or after a feeding, after every bowel movement, or when he or she might be uncomfortable because of a wet nappy.

Joan: I'll be so busy changing the baby I won't get time to change myself.

Doctor: You can do that when the baby's asleep. Let your baby snooze even if he's wet, unless he wakes up and cries. And be sure you clean him thoroughly every time you change his nappy. A good thing to use is sterile cotton wool or a little baby lotion. Then pat dry with a fresh towel, powder him thoroughly, especially in all the little crevices, and then put on a fresh nappy.

Joan: What should I do with the soiled nappies? Send them to the cleaners?

Doctor: No, and your laundry won't take them either. You'll have to wash them yourelf in your washing machine at home. Or else try using disposable nappies.

Joan: Maybe my parents can help me?

Doctor: Usually grandparents are very helpful. The baby often gives them a whole new lease of life. But don't let them or the baby disturb your routine. Try to keep the routine of your house as normal as possible. If you start out tiptoeing around and shushing everybody, your baby will grow up thinking the only normal environment is a Christian Science Reading Room.

Joan: Listen, what happens if my family or Edgar's hang around too much and try to take over the handling of my child?

Doctor: Put your foot down from the start. Remember, the child should have only one set of parents.

Joan: One visitor I'll be glad to see is my father.

Doctor: Is there any special reason?

Joan: Because my father is a doctor and you know what doctors are. They hate to make house calls. The other night my father was called at 4 a.m. by a hysterical woman who wouldn't stop screaming. So finally, he had to get out of bed and get dressed and go. He reckoned if my mother was that upset, he'd better go home.

Doctor: Well, for the routine problems with your baby you may not need a doctor. Just consult a good baby book. If the answer isn't there, then ring the doctor's

75

surgery. Have a pencil and paper ready to take down whatever he or she says.

Joan: My doctor usually says, 'Not you again, Miss Rivers.'

Doctor: A doctor will examine your baby very carefully before you leave hospital. Then it shouldn't be necessary for you to take him to the doctor for about six to eight weeks for another checkup. When you get home from hospital, the midwife will visit you, and later on, the health visitor. And it is wise to visit your local child health clinic regularly. These routine visits are important as they will help your doctor get to know your baby intimately.

Joan: And if the doctor's attractive, maybe they'll help me to get to know *him* intimately.

Doctor: Good afternoon, Miss Rivers. Next!

Who Is This Stranger in My Own Home? And Why Is He Making All These Impossible Demands on Me – and Never Once Has Said 'Thank You'?

I think I can truthfully say I had no idea that motherhood involved so much work. If it wasn't changing the nappies, it was sterilizing bottles, or mixing formulas – and all that screaming, grabbing, crying and upchucking – finally, I told Edgar, 'If you don't stop acting like this soon, I won't have any time for Melissa.'

Yes, Edgar was jealous, and although I never told him, I was delighted because by the time I had Melissa, we had been married three years and a lot of his ardour had cooled. I mean the only way I could get him jealous pre-baby was to take his secretary out to lunch. And believe me, I tried everything. I left cigar butts in all the bedroom ashtrays, army boots under my bed and shaving cream in the bathroom. His only comment was, 'Oh, is your Aunt Louise visiting us again?'

But now, suddenly all my time was being taken up by the baby – changing nappies, breast-feeding, bathing, laundering, lifting, dressing, lullabying. Whoever said it is more blessed to give than to receive must have been a bachelor – or sterile!

I remember talking to my doctor about this. I said:

Joan: Listen, don't you think giving the baby a bath every Saturday night along with the rest of us would be plenty?

Doctor: I think once a day would be better.

Joan: What should I bathe the baby in? When I was a kid, my mother used a tin bath.

Doctor: Who are you kidding? When you were a kid, you were dunked in the village well. Anyhow, you can sponge-bathe your baby on a table or in your lap. Or you can give him a bath in a washbowl, or a special baby bath, or even the kitchen sink – just make sure they are all scrubbed and rinsed out thoroughly beforehand.

Joan: Well, I can't use my kitchen sink. It's occupied all week until after Sunday dinner.

Doctor: With your dirty dishes?

Joan: No. With my maid. That's where she likes to sleep it off.

Doctor: Well, keep anyone who is not fully alert away from the baby at all times, especially during his bath when he is slippery and hard to hold. By the way, the best time to give the baby a bath is before you feed him. Afterwards he'll be ready to sleep.

Joan: Don't I know it! I always take a nap after I've been fed. It drives them crazy in McDonald's.

Doctor: I'd get the bath out of the way before the husband and father gets home.

Joan: Oh, that could never happen. They work on different shifts. And speaking of daddy coming home, how come a baby who has acted like an angel all day long suddenly sets up an unearthly howl at the exact moment when mummy chooses to fix herself up to look good for papa?

Doctor: It's called the 'rush hour syndrome'. The child senses the excitement and rushed preparations in the home before the father arrives.

Joan: Well, it isn't fair. Mothers should have time to fix themselves up. Otherwise, some husbands might start looking for a little extra-curricular activity. I mean, no man wants to make love to a wife wearing bunny slippers with one eye missing, an old towelling dressing gown and toilet paper wrapped around her hair.

Doctor: Is that what Edgar told you?

| Joan: | Edgar? He was late himself twice last week coming home from the office. I was furious. He claimed he'd been stuck in the rush hour traffic. |

Joan: Edgar? He was late himself twice last week coming home from the office. I was furious. He claimed he'd been stuck in the rush hour traffic.

Doctor: Maybe that's really so.

Joan: But he works upstairs. Actually, that's good as he'll be around the house a lot and will be able to help me with the baby. I understand that there are a couple of areas of a baby's body that require special attention.

Doctor: And so do a couple of yours.

Joan: Okay, so I'm not in such great shape. I'm still grateful.

Doctor: For what?

Joan: That wrinkles don't hurt. Now, back to baby. What are the special areas?

Doctor: Well for one, caring for the penis is quite easy. You simply retract the foreskin with each bath to keep it from adhering to the head of the penis. Of course, it is even easier to keep clean if the baby has been circumcised.

Joan: And simpler still if the baby's a girl.

Doctor: Incidentally, don't be surprised to see your baby with an erection. This occurs commonly when the bladder is full or baby is urinating. Something else that might be swollen on both boys and girls is their breasts.

Joan: It should only happen to me. I'm so flat-chested. I bought one of those cross-your-heart bras. Instead of separating and uplifting, it sent out a search party.

Doctor: Sometimes baby girls bleed from the vagina, but there is no reason for alarm, as both this and the swelling of the breasts happen to infants because the mother's hormones pass through the placenta into the baby's bloodstream.

Joan: Was it Aldous Huxley who said, 'Where the hormones, there moan I'? Any other special areas on my baby?

Doctor: The navel must be kept clean and dry. This means only sponge baths until the small cord drops off – which should be within ten days.

Joan: My cousin Natalie got out of that little duty nicely. She's been obsessed by how alienated kids are from their parents these days. So when she had her baby she refused to let the doctor cut the umbilical cord. 'Time enough when he gets married, God forbid,' she said. You never saw a closer relationship between a mother and son. They were inseparable. Of course, she found it tough to buy clothes.

Doctor: Speaking of clothes, when dressing your baby, less clothing is better than more.

Joan: That still is my theory – but I keep getting arrested.

Doctor: Mothers have always overdressed their babies and kept them bundled up no matter what the thermometer said.

Joan: You're telling me! One of the worst memories of my childhood is of the day my mother dressed me in a snowsuit, galoshes, woolly hat, scarf and mittens.

Doctor: Were you embarrassed?

Joan: You bet. I was the laughing stock of the beach.

Doctor: A good rule to follow is: dress your baby as you dress yourself. If it is cool and you need a sweater, then so does the baby. Actually, a fairly plump baby needs less covering than an adult. Also, a variety of temperatures helps the baby to toughen up and become adaptable. You know, of course, how beneficial sunlight is to children and adults alike. Expose him to the sun just a little bit at a time. Too much exposure can result in burns and injuries to your baby's skin.

Joan: If mummy's a day over 30, she won't be caught dead in direct sunlight. I personally always wear a hat with a heavy veil and I tell my friends I'm beekeeping. When should I take the kid out?

Doctor: By the time he's a couple of weeks old, the baby will be ready for his first pram ride. That'll be a great occasion for both you and the baby.

Joan: It sure will. If I can find somebody to push us. Ah, problems, problems.

Doctor: Come now, things aren't so bad. Look at all the adults around you. Once they were babies, and they came through.

Joan: Yeah, but sometimes I think how nice it would be if my kid just slept for the first couple of years. Then, presto! Baby would awake when he's maybe three years old, with the frustrations and torments of being a baby all behind him.

Doctor: For the first few months he may sleep an awful lot. Most babies are up for various periods. Others may sleep almost every minute they're not being fed, changed, or bathed. But only your baby can tell you how much sleep he needs.

Joan: I've never been able to understand a thing any person under six months tried to tell me. I wonder if there's a course at the Berlitz School that would help.

Doctor: Even a heavy sleeper will cut down to a nap or two during the day as he gets a little older. But it's best to get infants used to the idea that they go to sleep right after they've been fed.

Joan: Well, then I'll have a problem. Who should I put to bed first, the baby or Edgar?

Doctor: You should also try to get your baby used to falling asleep in his own bed, without company. And don't wake him up to show to your family and friends.

Joan: If you ask me, many babies shouldn't be shown even when they're awake. A friend of mine had a kid who was really ugly. Once he fell in the gutter and the cop who found him called the RSPCA.

Doctor: After the first six months or so, the baby will probably give you a break in the morning by sleeping later.

Joan: Do you think with a lot of love and coaxing he could stretch that to noon?

Doctor: To 6 a.m., if you're lucky. But believe me, when you open your eyes and see him lying there on his tummy –

Joan: On his tummy?

Doctor: Yes. Most babies seem to prefer to lie on their tummies.

Joan: Which makes them cleverer than a lot of mummies, who'd have been better off if they'd kept lying on their tummies.

Doctor: Incidentally, after six months, the baby should be moved out of your bedroom at night. When a child reaches that age, he's old enough to sleep on his own. Also, it's best not to take the baby into your bed at night for any reason.

Joan: No matter how helpless and frightened mummy might be feeling?

Doctor: Relax. Be cool. Have fun with baby.

Joan: Doctor, it was 'having fun' that brought me baby. God knows what having more fun might lead to.

Doctor: You should let your baby know it's a joy having him. Talk to him and don't make caring for him a drag. You can be serious about being a good mother

without being grim and tense about it. When the baby's awake, it wants companionship. But that doesn't mean you have to be its constant buddy. Sometime, let him help amuse himself. Give him things to play with that are safe. But remember that everything will end up in his mouth, so keep small objects that he can easily swallow away from him.

Joan: That's easy to do when he's in the cot but what about when he gets older?

Doctor: Well, when you have the time to watch him, let him crawl around on his own and investigate his surroundings. But when you're busy, it's best to put him in a playpen. That way he can be where you are and see what you're up to.

Joan: Mummy's sometimes up to plenty she's just as soon not have baby spying on. Besides, I've heard playpens aren't such a good idea for babies.

Doctor: That's true. Many doctors feel that they keep a baby from becoming adventurous and exploring new territory, but the playpen can be a great boon, especially for the busy mother. When he's old enough to stand up, baby can hang on to the railing and feel the terra firma under him.

Joan: How can I help my kid get around before he starts to move on his own?

Doctor: A baby-walker or a swing is a pleasant and useful device for the baby in that interval between learning to sit up and starting to crawl . . . and speaking of crawling, Miss Rivers, if you want another appointment you'd better be a *lot* nicer.

CHAPTER IX

If He Hollers . . . Let Him Go!

*T*HE only thing I couldn't get over with Melissa was the amount of time she spent crying. But when I say cry, I don't mean cry, I mean CRY. The last person I'd seen cry like that was Edgar on our wedding night. And it seemed like she would never stop and it really upset me. I mean, what has a baby got to cry about? It's amused and fondled and cuddled and bubbled and coo-cooed at all day long. If Edgar paid even half that attention to me, I'd give up kissing my pillow. I mean, how do you put a silencer on a squawk box? I tried everything to keep her quiet; I sang soothingly to her, I fed her, changed her nappy. Nothing helped. She just kept on screaming. Finally, I threatened that if she didn't stop crying, I'd never come near her again. That was the first time I ever saw Melissa sit up, laugh and clap her hands. And that started me crying! You know something, there's nothing like a good cry. I remember what my doctor told me:

Doctor: Babies cry because they're hungry or uncomfortable or need exercise. Again, the operative word is: relax. You'll learn how to adjust the feeds to your baby's needs.

Joan: Well, what if he's fed and is still crying his head off, and I've already changed his nappy 13 times? There's nothing more to come out. Is the kid sick? Has he got a safety pin jabbing him somewhere I can't see? Can it be fatigue? How could it be when he's been on his back in his cot all day long? And it can't be loneliness either as mummy's been lying right there beside him.

Doctor: You may have a fretful baby. Try to find the cause. Or it may be just a stage.

Joan: The whole world's a stage. And we poor mothers are but stagehands. What should I do to stop the crying?

Doctor: Try wrapping the baby cosily in a shawl. Maybe a dummy between feeds. Or some music.

Joan: Great, and if none of these things work on me, I'll try them on the baby.

Doctor: If the baby screams his head off at about the same time every day, chances are the baby has colic. This usually comes after a feed and is probably due to a cramping of the intestines. It's fairly commonplace. It too will pass. Don't panic. Remember, when you pick up the colicky baby to soothe him, he may scream harder than ever.

Joan: My mother was right. She loved to quote Shakespeare to my sister and me when we were growing up. Her favourite passage was from *King Lear*: 'How sharper than the serpent's tooth is the thankless child!' Her dentist taught her that.

SEYMOUR XAVIER SCHAINHOLZ, M.D.

Dear Joanie,

You are one busy girl! It seems every time I hear you on the Tonight Show you're getting ready to open in Las Vegas or Miami Beach or Chicago or wherever. It was lovely to hear that you take Missy and the nurse with you when you travel. You seem to be always on the go.

I can well imagine your mail has a hard time catching up with you-- and that a lot of it just plain gets lost in transit. So please forgive me for resubmitting my statement for bringing Missy into the world.

All best wishes for your continued success,

Dear Joan,

I heard you joking the other day on the Merv Griffin Show about how inefficient your secretary is. You said you had dictated a letter that morning and the secretary asked you, "Does it have to get out this year?"

I can well imagine such a secretary is pretty sloppy about handling your mail. Who knows, she probably loses half of it and fails to bring the other half to your attention.

Therefore, please be understanding about my writing "Personal" on the envelope. You'll notice I didn't write "Urgent!" (ha, ha!) and that I took the liberty of enclosing a stamped, self-addressed envelope for you to use.

Most respectfully yours,

93

Doctor: If you get angry with the baby – and you will – just bear in mind the baby isn't consciously trying to upset you. He's just a little pile of parts and nerve endings and doesn't realize he's upsetting you. Admit you're angry and try to share a good laugh about it with your husband.

Joan: I'll have to find him first.

Doctor: Well, I can understand why you're tense, and the tension will only increase if you've got one of those real problemy, colicky, crying babies. You've got to think a little about yourself and your own sanity, too. Try to make some kind of arrangement where you can get away for three or four hours a day or at least twice a week, as every mother needs a relief shift – and her husband is as good a bet as any.

Joan: Or anyone's husband for that matter but, to tell you the truth, I don't really trust my husband with the kid. I think he'll try to spoil him.

Doctor: More often than not, it's the mother who does the spoiling.

Joan: Well, believe me, I won't spoil my kid. No fancy cars, or separate suites – 'til he's toilet trained.

Doctor: There are other ways to spoil a child.

Joan: By leaving him out in the rain and letting him rust?

Doctor: No. It could be that you've tried too strenuously to amuse your baby. If you have, the baby will be clamouring for fun and games from mummy all day long, and mummy will soon find the entertainment burden intolerable.

Joan: I've sometimes heard that same comment from my audiences.

Doctor: It's natural to spoil the first-born a little. Parenthood is a new game for mummy and daddy. The baby's the greatest thing that ever happened to them. They feel all this responsibility toward the helpless little bundle, and understandably they may overreact to the crying. But there are certain types who are more likely to spoil their babies. Take a person like yourself. Someone who's – what is the best way to put it – well, slightly older than springtime.

Joan: That was not the best way to put it. Besides, I'm 23.

Doctor: How can that be?

Joan: I don't count when I sleep.

Doctor: Because you waited so long to have your baby you might tend to give in to your baby's every demand. This is typical of older parents. You must stop and remind yourself that the baby doesn't have sense enough to know what's good for it.

Joan: Neither do I.

Doctor: Well, you'd better try and work it out. And, frankly, if I were you, I'd enjoy this period now when you are the 'boss' of your baby. Pretty soon, at about four years of age, he'll be questioning your every decision.

Joan: And probably winning.

Doctor: Ah – but only if you've let him win from the start. So don't let him. Just make up your mind that you're going to go about your normal routine most of the time your baby is awake.

Joan: That means I'll have to take the baby on the nightclub stage with me. Actually, it might be just the gimmick my act's been needing for a long time.

95

Doctor:	Just don't turn him into a little tyrant of the night by letting him bully you with his crying. If you pick him up at night and start walking him when he sets up a howl, he'll have you walking all night long. Another nice little trick a spoiled baby uses to command attention is to vomit when he gets in a fury.
Joan:	Shouldn't a mother get worried? I mean, if I were doing it, I know my kid would be upset.
Doctor:	Actually, vomiting and drooling and spitting up are common with babies. So just relax. Another thing many babies do is thumb-sucking. Everyone has a theory about it. Whether it's good or bad. Whether it should be tolerated or discouraged.
Joan:	I'm against thumb-sucking. Only when everything else has failed and all entreaties to reason have been ignored, do I personally resort to it.
Doctor:	A baby sucks his thumb mainly because he hasn't had enough of a go at the breast or the bottle to satisfy his sucking need. I think it might be an inherent trait that runs strong in some families and skips others altogether.
Joan:	It certainly runs in my family. My cousin Shirley is 21 and is still a thumb-sucker.
Doctor:	You mean to tell me a 21-year-old girl still sucks her thumb?
Joan:	Not hers. Other people's. Poor thing. She goes crazy every time she sees a hitchhiker.
Doctor:	Well, she's not unusual. Most thumb-suckers get started before they're three months old and usually phase it out by the time they're six or seven months old. If they're still sucking after that, they're doing it to soothe themselves and not to satisfy a sucking

need. It's my own personal theory that a breast-fed baby is less likely to become a thumb-sucker. That's because his mummy will probably let him suck to his little heart's content. But when a bottle's empty, it's empty, and baby doesn't get a big charge out of sucking air.

Joan: Listen, I've heard of many a baby that went straight from mummy's nipple to his own thumb.

Doctor: Then maybe his mother should have let him suck longer – a half hour or more if it's convenient.

Joan: It most certainly is not convenient. The way my day is programmed, I'd have to be breast-feeding while I'm at the supermarket, cooking, cleaning, running errands, walking the dog . . .

Doctor: You could shorten that time if at each feeding you let it have both breasts.

Joan: At this point, I'd like to let it have both barrels. Is it true that thumb-sucking is bad for the teeth?

Doctor: A lot of parents worry about this and they really shouldn't, as long as the child has kicked the habit by the time he's five or six years old when his permanent teeth are coming along.

Joan: My Aunt Helga looks like a sabre-toothed tiger. Her teeth jut out so straight she can hang clothes from them. But then she's 48 and still sucking. At first her parents tried to stop her, but they couldn't. And besides, having prominent upper teeth has its advantages. She can walk in the rain and never get her chin wet.

Doctor: If you've got a thumb-sucker, don't be a nag. And avoid any restraints like mitts, or putting horrible-tasting stuff on the thumb. This will only frustrate

the child. Many mothers nip the thumb-sucking habit in the bud with a dummy.

Joan: But you have to buy that. The thumb's cheaper. Another nice thing about a thumb is it doesn't keep falling on the floor. You don't have to keep sterilizing it, either. Besides, who wants to push a kid around who looks like it's got a corkscrew stuck in its mouth?

Doctor: The 'plus' of a dummy is that most babies will kick the habit when they're five or six months old. Whereas a thumb-sucker doesn't kick his until he's three or four years old or older. Besides the dummy or thumb, when a baby is six months old he begins to reach for other comforts like his blanket.

Joan: And when he's sixteen, he reaches for who's under the blanket.

Doctor: A baby is about six months old when he first begins to realize he is a person in his own right and not just an extension of mummy. For some reason the other comforters that he picks – like a cuddly toy or nappy or blanket – are usually dirty. In fact, the dirtier and mangier the object, the greater can be the baby's devotion to it. There's really not much that you should do about it.

Joan: Except to put the kid and the comforter through a car wash once a month.

Doctor: The best thing to do is not to fight it. Try to clean the object, whatever it is, when baby's not looking. Or palm off a clean duplicate on him. But don't be surprised if he doesn't fall for the ruse. In any case, the child should give up this crutch, too, in good time.

Joan: Easy for you to say. My cousin Rebecca had an old blanket she adored. She carried it everywhere with her – even when she was grown up – and it caused a lot of comment. Maybe because it was a king-size electric job.

Doctor: Oh, one other thing that you should take in your stride is any head-banging or rocking in the cot.

Joan: But what if the baby is beating his brains out?

Doctor: This would not be a common occurrence but in such a case you should seek help from a doctor. Except in rare instances, however, the baby is just beginning to develop a sense of rhythm.

Joan: You're speaking of black babies, of course. I'm Jewish, so I don't have to worry. None of us have any rhythm. And neither do a lot of Catholics, from the sizes of some of their families.

Doctor: Well, take whatever rhythm you have and dance out of here.

CHAPTER X

A Growing Baby May Be Hazardous to Mummy's Health and Nerves

As Melissa grew, I was delighted to see that she was bright – all things considered. I mean she was no genius like my sister's little boy who was so clever that when the rest of the kids sat in the sandpit and made patty cakes, he made soil tests. But she wasn't a thickhead like the kid next door who when she took her first step, took it backwards.

The thing that I had to keep remembering was that each child is unique and has its own tempo. For example, Melissa didn't learn to eat with a fork 'til she was, say, past two, while my cousin's kid was less than eighteen months old when she first used her fork. The entire restaurant turned around to watch in amazement as such a young child – completely unaided – picked up her fork all by herself and stuck it into her new baby brother.

Of course, although I hated to admit it, one of the reasons I expected Melissa to be clever was because my family has never had any slow developers (outside of the girls in the chest area). My mother says I was the first kid in our street to put on her shoes and socks. Unfortunately, I put them on in that order.

Relax and let your baby develop his motor skills at his own rate. And once he gets such things as holding his head erect, sitting, standing, crawling and walking in that order, you can look forward to the next stage of development, which in Melissa's case included lighting my cigar, tickling my back and refilling my glass.

I still can hear my doctor telling me . . .

Doctor:	There's little connection between a child's intelligence and how fast he acquires these skills. When we learn to stand, walk or whatever, our rate of progress has to do mainly with hereditary factors.
Joan:	What about intelligence? Does that depend on heredity also?
Doctor:	Intelligence has more to do with environment, which is why I'm already worried about your child.
Joan:	How soon can you tell how bright a baby is?
Doctor:	Well, for the first two or three months the baby's almost totally wrapped up in himself.
Joan:	I know some babies who went on to spend the next 70 or 80 years being all wrapped up in themselves.
Doctor:	After about three months, he's ready to discover the world. In getting a grip on this little body of his, he starts by using his head.
Joan:	Doctor, you and I both know that's the last thing anybody ever uses.
Doctor:	Baby can tell light from dark the moment he's born. In a few weeks yours will be recognizing your face and responding to it.
Joan:	By screaming his bloody head off.
Doctor:	Keep smiling. He'll start imitating you. That's how he begins developing into a friendly, social being.

Joan: Not by imitating my smile, I can assure you.

Doctor: Gradually, after two or three months he learns how to use his hands, too, until he gets pretty good at it. Before he's a year old, he'll delight in picking up the tiniest of things, like a speck of dust.

Joan: Great! Then I can fire my cleaning lady. Doctor, I don't want to complain, but she is the worst. She swept so much dust under my rug, we have to walk uphill to get to the kitchen.

Doctor: Miss Rivers, knowing your panic level, there's something I'd like to clarify. Parents tend to panic at the thought of a left-handed child. Which way the baby will go is not an inherited trait. He may go one way for awhile and then the other. A lot of babies straddle the fence for the first year or so and stay ambidextrous.

Joan: And 21 years later, they're AC/DC?

Doctor: The point is, do not force your child to use either hand. Let him use the hand that is most comfortable for him – and the same goes with other skills. The age at which a baby learns to roll, sit up, stand up, and walk varies a lot. Temperament and weight have much to do with it. A fat baby may not have much of a yen to get moving very fast.

Joan: Don't I know it. I was such a fat baby I had barely reached the sitting up stage when it was time for me to go to school. My parents took me there in a wheelbarrow. And by the time I got married, I was so fat, they had to roll me down the aisle.

Doctor: But you're so thin now, how did you accomplish that?

Joan: I just eat my own cooking.

Doctor: Well, if your baby does the same, he'll probably be thin and an early mover. Babies start crawling any time between six months and a year. But some never crawl at all. They just sit around until they're ready to stand up.

Joan: I'd just as soon that any child of mine skipped the crawling phase.

Doctor: A hot-shot baby might start walking at nine months. Most babies start between a year and 15 months. But many an intelligent, healthy baby doesn't take a step until he's 18 months or more.

Joan: If he was really intelligent, he'd put it off a lot longer and keep conning mummy into hauling and pushing him.

Doctor: Some mummies are apt to force the walking issue, and this is a big mistake. The baby will start to walk when it's ready to, without any parental prodding.

Joan: So I shouldn't try to help the baby by putting training wheels on him?

Doctor: Mothers who try to force their children to walk before they are ready can actually delay progress. And mothers who 'help' the baby to walk by constantly holding his hands and sort of swinging him across the room are really not helping him learn. This kind of subsidized walking can become too much fun for the baby to drop for the real thing.

Joan: Does the same apply to talking?

Doctor: And how! If there's any pressure on a baby to get talking, he may just decide to clam up. Usually, when babies are about a year old they are just making sounds that mean something – not actually words.

Joan: When should a woman start to panic?

Doctor: It's hard to say. When a child really begins to talk is mostly a matter of personality. An extrovertish type wants to get his two pence worth in early. But the strong, silent type may take a long, cool look at the world around him before feeling any utterances coming on. Also, talking at the pace of a tobacco auctioneer as you do, Miss Rivers, your baby may have trouble being able to copy single words. Slow down. One word at a time.

Joan: And if the word keeps coming back to you as 'grr' or 'ki-ki', at what point do you really know you're the proud mother of a stupid child?

Doctor: You can't use speech as a gauge. Some very bright children don't talk much before three. Try not to get tense about it. Talk to your baby in a friendly way, using simple words, and try to coax him into asking for things by their name.

Joan: In other words, if my kid wants me he should call me, 'Miss Rivers'?

Doctor: Your kid is going to want you a lot during teething, but you can't win any superiority sweepstakes because your baby teethed early. It proves nothing. The timing has to do with the baby's rate of bodily development.

Joan: I've always been told you can use it as an all-purpose cop-out. Your baby's screaming 24 hours a day and he throws up on Grandma anytime she picks him up. You just say, 'He's teething.'

Doctor: Too many things are blamed on teething that shouldn't be.

Joan: Like my wedding night.

Doctor: The average baby gets its first tooth around six

110

months and continues teething for most of his first two and a half years. In that time he will get 20 teeth.

Joan: That's the same rate that I'm losing mine. Every time I hear the song 'Bridge Over Troubled Waters', I think it refers to me.

Doctor: Much as it might disturb your aesthetic or hygienic sense, reconcile yourself to the fact that the baby's going to be chewing on everything it can get into its mouth.

Joan: Well, if it's chewing on mummy, it'll be chewing the fat.

Doctor: Better that he chew a rubber ring or something of the sort. And keep the baby away from thin celluloid toys and anything that's been repainted at home.

Joan: Thank God! That means my face is off-limits. Listen, Doc, what gives a child good teeth? I had bad teeth from the start. I lost so many teeth at once when I was a kid, the tooth fairy got a hernia.

Doctor: It depends a lot on what the mother ate during pregnancy, and the diet the baby is on after birth.

Joan: When do my baby's permanent teeth start forming?

Doctor: Just a few months after birth. Though they don't start putting in an appearance until he's six years old.

Joan: And I'll bet the dentists can't wait. I know my dentist made a fortune on me.

Doctor: The best way to avoid cavities is to avoid sweets. They really are the diggers of holes in children's teeth. If it's humanly possible, try to keep sweets away from your baby.

Joan: It's easier said than done. What kind of a mother can resist her kid's tears and won't share her lollipop or liquorice stick with her own flesh and blood? I mean, I've even seen my dentist's wife slipping her kid sweets.

Doctor: I'm truly surprised at that.

Joan: Well, they're a strange couple. We once went out to dinner with them. As soon as we sat down, he clipped my napkin around my neck, shoved two little cotton hot dogs in my mouth and when my martini came, he made me take a sip, swirl it around and spit it out!

CHAPTER XI

The First Year Is the Hardest – Until the Second Year

I never thought I'd say it, but by the time Melissa reached one year I began to realize that when a mother referred to 'the good old days', she was talking about her baby's first few months. All that happened then was Melissa ate, slept, smiled and screamed, and I was in control.

Then came her first birthday and it was all over. She wanted to go poking into everything, try everything, investigate everything. For all normal babies suddenly turn into explorers and nobody can tell them they aren't Marco Polo, Magellan, Christopher Columbus and Edmund Hillary combined – except maybe their psychiatrists when they're 21!

So, I had to let Melissa go, for nothing I could do or say could dampen her sense of adventure. Pulling, pushing, feeling, kicking, she simply had to put her touch on everything, and that was healthy. One can be a dangerous age (but then so can 17). To make my house safer I took a whole series of common-place precautions.

I put harnesses on highchairs and in Melissa's push chair. Guards went on all the upstairs windows and a safety gate in front of the stairs. Luckily I didn't have to take special care to keep Melissa from getting burned in our kitchen. She never went near it. She hated my cooking so much right from the start that at ten months she taught herself how to phone the Chinese takeaway. So be careful. I remember my doctor's first words of caution to me . . .

Doctor: Keep far out of reach all tiny objects like buttons, beads, peanuts, beans, pins, etc., that the baby might put in his mouth and which could get lodged in his windpipe.

Joan: Something really teensy-tiny, though, might go right down? Like the diamond on mummy's engagement ring?

Doctor: Electric flexes should be in top condition. And sockets that are not used should be plugged up so baby won't be tempted to jam things into them. Keep dangerous tools out of sight. Matches also should be kept out of baby's reach. Swimming pools and wells should be fenced off. Put a life jacket on the baby whenever he's near water, and put him in a special child's car seat when he's in the car. Keep him from being exposed to anything with a cutting edge. Opened tin cans, broken glass . . .

Joan: . . . his Grandma's tongue.

Doctor: Used razor blades should go back into their container.

Joan: That's a great excuse for me to stop shaving.

Doctor: Go through your house from stem to stern and tuck · everything away that's potentially poisonous. All medicines and insecticides and cleaning materials and polishes and sprays and detergents and rat poisons and petrol and paraffin and turpentine and the like. Be sure to put all pills safely out of reach. Babies seem to have a special yen for pills – maybe because they see you take them and want to imitate mummy.

Joan: Because of this my cousin gave up the pill. She practised the rhythm method for five years and ended up with four kids who are great tap dancers.

Doctor: This is the age when a baby might be both frightened and fascinated by strange objects that make sudden loud noises, like trains or planes or the whirring of a blender or a power lawnmower or the barking of a dog. Shield him as best you can from these disturbances. If the running of a vacuum cleaner should frighten him, give up using it in front of him for a few months.

Joan: If the running of the vacuum cleaner doesn't frighten him, what measures can I take to see that it does?

Doctor: Also, at this age, the bath can suddenly become terrifying. If a big bath frightens him, use something smaller, like a baby bath, or get special toys for the bath. There are special soap crayons most children like, as they can paint themselves and get clean at the same time.

Joan: All kids I know love their baths. My sister's little boy giggles and laughs from the time she puts him in the washing machine until he's spun dry.

Doctor: Remember, this is the time for letting the baby try his wings. His journey to freedom and independence begins with a crawl – all the way to another room. Soon he can walk, and when he can walk, don't keep him secured in his pushchair. He needs his daily constitutionals. Don't let him wander off and put sand and dirt in his mouth, of course, but it's perfectly healthy for him to get dirty.

Joan: With all this crawling and walking, I guess it's bye-bye playpen?

Doctor: Yes, now it's going to be hard to keep him out of trouble and in the pen. And pretty soon you're going to have to let him have the run of the house.

Joan: Hey wait a minute, that's a prerogative my mother still doesn't let me have. To this day I've never been in her living room. I just stand at the entrance and admire it over the rope.

Doctor: Your mother was probably afraid that you'd break things. You can prevent this . . .

Joan: by handcuffing the child . . .

Doctor: by putting the really rare and lovely things out of his reach and putting interesting alternatives in their places. Besides, a child of one can be taught not to do

118

certain things such as touch a hot stove, turn on the gas, pull lamps off the tables by their flexes . . .

Joan: . . . or wake mummy before noon.

Doctor: Just get ready to say 'no' over and over again and say it like you mean it, firmly but cheerfully. Also distract him if you can with something allowable that he's apt to find as interesting as the forbidden object.

Joan: If laryngitis starts coming on before those thousand no's are said, how about one giant 'Shove off'?

Doctor: Blowing your cool will accomplish nothing. Yelling, scolding, dirty looks, finger waving will not do the job. He'll either have to give in meekly or go on defying you.

Joan: What's wrong about giving in meekly? After all, 'Blessed are the meek for they shall inherit the earth.' A probate judge told me that.

Doctor: Bullying a baby into submission is bad for the development of his personality. So control yourself. You'll have to prevail, but do it with good humour, without arguments or scoldings, no matter if he kicks and screams his bloody little head off. Deep down, he'll feel good knowing that you're doing what has to be done without getting cross.

Joan: It's hard being a mother.

Doctor: It's harder being a baby. Think how big everyone and everything looks to him – and how frightening it must be when visitors swoop down and try to hug and kiss him. Babies need time to size up strangers before getting chummy. Often when people pounce on the baby, he'll cry and retreat back to mummy. When this happens, just say, 'The baby's a little shy.'

119

Joan: But mummy's not shy and would love to be pounced on.

Doctor: Something else you'd better be prepared for is the time when the baby starts dropping things. Not to annoy you. He's doing this dropping and throwing on purpose because it's a big new achievement for him. He'll be pleased as anything to have you returning the things to him. That makes it a two-person game, but it's best not to make a habit of picking up the things he's dropping.

120

Joan: But won't the health visitor have something to say about that? I mean, with the piles of mashed bananas and wet cereal and boiled eggs mounting up on my floor?

Doctor: I was referring to his toys. When a baby gets into a dropping mood, put him on the floor. Or tie his toys to his pram or his highchair with short pieces of string.

Joan: What if he starts throwing his food? My friend Mary's kid did that, but she didn't get cross. She knew he was just imitating his father.

Doctor: A baby won't start throwing his food 'til he's pretty full. At this point take the food away and just let him play. And by the way, it's at this age he'll start getting much choosier.

Joan: I know. Mary told me. Once she had prepared a great meal for her kid – lamb chops, spinach, mashed potatoes and ice cream – and he wouldn't touch it. She was so upset. It had taken her hours to stuff all that into the bottle.

Doctor: At one, a baby often isn't as hungry as he was. Teething may have something to do with it. So don't force-feed. He's entitled to his personal preferences in food. From the start, try to act sensibly about feeding and you won't have problems later on. Get across the notion that eating is enjoyable.

Joan: In my house that will be easy. I'll just smile and say, 'Eat some more, love. It's good. Mummy didn't make it.'

Doctor: As long as you're offering a good selection of wholesome foods, don't worry about how much or how little he may eat at one meal. Or if he seems to be addicted to avocados one week and won't touch

121

them the next. And if your child is a poor eater, games will help distract him.

Joan: My father used to play airport with me. The food was the plane and my mouth was the hangar. He'd say, 'Here comes the plane into the hangar.' I loved that game. I even made up my own version. It was called 'Spit the plane in the pilot's eye.' When will my baby be able to feed himself?

Doctor: That depends mostly on the parent's attitude. Some babies can do a pretty good job of spoon-feeding themselves before they're a year old. Then you'll hear a certain kind of mother say that her two-year-old couldn't conceivably feed himself.

Joan: Well, we all know what kind of a mother that is. She and her darling little Herbie will be spooning together down through the years.

Doctor: A baby can take his first step towards self-feeding when he's only six months old and he's allowed to hold some finger foods.

Joan: In my house, all foods are finger foods. I figure, if God wanted us to use utensils, our hands would be silver plated.

Doctor: 'Twixt the spoon and the lip there's many a slip, however. The baby who thinks that if his parents can use a spoon he surely can is in for a rude surprise. The first few hundred tries he'll find that for every particle of food that reaches his mouth, 99 others have fallen on himself or the floor. But don't help him out. Let him have a go at it. At the beginning of a meal, he'll be hungry enough to persist. The more adept he gets at feeding himself, the longer you should let him stick with it.

Joan: Until one meal just kind of blends into the next?

122

Doctor: He'll get so he can knock off something he really likes in ten or fifteen minutes. At that point don't start spoon-feeding him the other things he should be eating. In his young mind that will set up a distinction between what he wants and what you want to get into him. And by all means don't fret about table manners. Believe me, the baby wants to be neater and cleaner as fast as he can manage it.

123

Joan: Table manners worry everyone. Which fork to use with what? I have a rule, just start with the thing farthest away on your left and work in towards your plate.

Doctor: That sounds logical.

Joan: Except for the time I found myself trying to eat soup with a napkin.

Doctor: One last thing. About the age of one, your baby may be giving up his morning nap. The baby that snoozed so regularly at 9 a.m. may start putting off that nap until it runs into the lunch hour. In that case, serve an early lunch. Lunch will probably go immediately into a long nap.

Joan: All this talk of bed reminded me I have to return my water bed. I bought it strictly for sex, but my husband stocked it with trout. So long, Doc.

CHAPTER XII

Going Potty, or Accidents Will Happen

ONCE your baby has some teeth, is crawling about and is able to say a few words, it's the time (hooray) to housebreak him.

Every mother has her own method. Mine was the applause gimmick. Melissa and I got off to a great start with this. Every day I would put her on the potty and when she had done what I wanted I would applaud her efforts. Just like the books said, I did this for several weeks and I was beginning to feel quite confident. Then Melissa got things backwards, and whenever the television was on and she heard applause, she did a wee . . . in the living room.

A friend of mine who trains dogs tried to apply the same methods she used to her child. She used to hit him over the nose with a rolled up newspaper the same as she did with her puppies. But it didn't work out. By the time her baby was three, he still wasn't trained, although he had learned to fetch, beg and roll over.

I hate to brag, but Melissa learned very quickly. I'll never forget the day she was finally trained. It was quite an event. Not only did it mean the end of all the messiness and dirty nappies, but it even had a greater significance: it meant the end of my affair with the nappy man.

However, all this was a long time after my first discussion with the doctor about toilet training . . .

Joan:	Tell me, Doc, when can I start training my kid? I trained the dog at two months.
Doctor:	When your youngster is old enough to learn the hang of it and physically able to bring it off.
Joan:	That's too bad. In my cousin Shirley's case it wasn't until she was 14.
Doctor:	Some babies can sit on the potty in the latter part of the first year. The kind of baby to put there will be the one who usually has a bowel movement a few minutes after breakfast every day. That way the mother can predictably 'catch' his movement.
Joan:	That's what I call a regular baby.
Doctor:	You can't expect baby to be conscious of what's happening there on the toilet seat. But after a few weeks of this he may sense that the moment he gets the seat under him is the time to start pushing.
Joan:	May I have the pushiest kid on the block!
Doctor:	This early start, as I said, can be all to the good. But the baby who is 'regular' is cooperating unknowingly. Later, when he's wise to what's been happening, he may clam up and resist. But after the first year things start looking up. The baby becomes aware of his bowel movements, and he takes a possessive attitude towards them.
Joan:	That's your definition of things 'looking up'?
Doctor:	And he'll be so proud of what he's done – whether it's in his nappy or in his potty. Sure as anything, he'll want to show it to mummy.
Joan:	I can't believe my life. I'm bankrupting myself to buy flowers and art reproductions in order to create a

truly beautiful environment for him, and the kid wants me to look at bowel movements.

Doctor: Soon after he's a year old, he'll go through a couple of phases that will indicate he's ripe for toilet training. Neither one will seem to be directly related to bowel movements – but they are. You'll notice that he becomes a very giving little person. For instance, if you have a friend who's visiting, he'll drag out all his toys and make presents of them to her. This shows his pleasure in parting with something and getting mummy's approval for a grown-up gesture. Then you'll notice how intrigued he gets with putting things into containers. He might also start alerting mummy with some special gesture or noise when he feels a movement coming on. When you do catch the movement, it's an occasion for rejoicing and congratulating the baby on acting like a big boy or big girl.

Joan: If he wants to act really grown-up, he'll learn how to be constipated.

Doctor: Be prepared for relapses during this period. The baby between one and one and a half years old who seems to have the hang of using the potty may suddenly balk. He'll hold everthing in as long as he's on the potty and let go the minute he's off.

Joan: I have an idea. I'll show him who's boss. I'll strap his little behind to the potty and say, 'Now you're not moving until you move.'

Doctor: That's precisely what not to do. Don't keep him on the potty more than five or ten minutes at a time, regardless of the results. If nothing happens, don't let your frustration show, for by the second half of the second year most babies are aware that a poo is coming, and they'll actually notify you when the great moment is at hand.

Joan: Oh, how I long to hear those three little words.

Doctor: 'I love you'?

Joan: No. 'Gotta go potty.'

Doctor: Up to the time he's maybe two or two and a half years old, the baby is probably better off on his own small potty than on a seat that fits on the toilet. He'll be able to mount his little throne without any help from you, and he'll be proud to have his own little piece of furniture. However, it's a good idea to wait until he's left the bathroom before emptying the potty into the toilet and flushing it.

Joan: Good heavens, you'd think the kid was Howard Hughes. You know he never went to the toilet. He hired four faceless peasants to go for him.

Doctor: The reason for not flushing in front of the baby is that some babies get frightened by the sudden torrents of water. Don't introduce him to his potty cold turkey. Let him do some dry runs on it – let him get used to his potty just as if it were a new plaything. Let him have some fun, while sitting on it fully clothed. Then, subtly – or not so subtly – you can sneak in the commercial: 'This is your very own potty in which you can have a poo. Like big people do on the big toilet.' And one fine day –

Joan: One fine day, baloney. Remember, Doctor, you can lead a baby to potty but you can't make him poo.

Doctor: Nevertheless, by the time he's eighteen months old I think you should start trying, whether or not baby seems so inclined. Consider it your responsibility to –

Joan:	I know – to make his business *my* business.
Doctor:	Even at this stage a youngster is most apt to let mummy know *after* the fact. But cheer up. This is still a sign of progress.
Joan:	You have the most perverse definitions of progress.
Doctor:	While you're cleaning him up, keep telling him that there's a better, more grown-up way of doing things and that's to do them into the potty. During the second half of the child's second year, you'll get a boost from his natural inclination to imitate and please his parents.
Joan:	An inclination that quickly passes, no doubt.
Doctor:	If it's a first-born, he won't, of course, have a big brother or sister to watch. Most authorities seem agreed it isn't good for him to watch his parents on the toilet.
Joan:	Together? I'll bet that's one even Havelock Ellis never heard of.
Doctor:	He's not going to learn in a few days or even weeks, and you've got to be his patient, cheerful and optimistic guide.
Joan:	I have a great idea. What if I keep him on a liquid diet 'til he gets the hang of it.
Doctor:	Be a little firm when you think he knows what he should be doing and is stalling. But no nagging or sermonizing, and don't be above a little harmless bribery. Like promising some new clothes or a wanted dolly when the feat is accomplished.
Joan:	So, that's why my husband's training is perfect.
Doctor:	As soon as the baby can stay clean part of the time, you can get him out of nappies and into training pants. This is a big leap forward psychologically.

131

Joan: The only big leap forward I'm interested in is the one that lands him on the toilet seat in time.

Doctor: Then, voilà! One happy day you find you can depend on baby to let you know when he's ready for action. But he still expects you to take down his pants and get him on the seat. He can do both these jobs for himself when he's about three. And he can begin wiping himself. By the time he's two and a half years old, he should be trying his hand at this, if you'll forgive the expression.

Joan: So far we've been talking just about bowel movements. I hate to sound show biz, Doc, but to quote the song: 'Another opening, another flow.'

Doctor: Urine training can be a tougher job than bowel movement training.

Joan: Thanks, Doctor, I really needed that to complete my day.

Doctor: It seems to go more slowly anyway – especially for boys. Most two-year-olds have pretty much mastered bowel movements, but plenty of two-and-a-half-year-olds are still moist little people, because for eighteen months or so a baby's bladder flushes itself almost automatically. But then, one glorious day the mother discovers her baby has been dry up to two hours.

Joan: To think such happiness could be mine!

Doctor: But it's not because the baby's going into training. It's just that the bladder is maturing.

Joan: This is the time to hire a wet nurse, right?

Doctor: I suggest that you put him on the potty every two hours. His bladder should be full by then so he won't have to be enthroned too long. Place him there in the morning as soon as he wakes up, before and after naps and meals, and after he's been dry for two hours.

Joan: And sing him 'Tinkle, tinkle, little star.'

Doctor: Potty training is not an Olympic feat. There shouldn't be any sense of competitiveness with other children. Parents shouldn't compare their child's progress with that of other people's babies.

Joan: But what else do you talk about with other mothers? You're in that park and you hear some mum bragging, 'My little Suzy's only nine months old, but she's a perfect lady the way she takes care of her private functions.' Well, you've just got to find a topper. Like, 'My Johnny not only takes care of himself, but he helps his father zip up.'

Doctor: Years from now, you won't be able to remember just how long it took. But it will matter if the training was carried out with love and patience and a bond of mutual trust was established between you and the baby at this time.

Joan: I was rather hoping the bond would come about through a shared appreciation of gourmet cooking, literature and good music.

Doctor: Incidentally the well-trained child of, say, two sometimes gets so conditioned to his own potty that he can't perform anywhere else. Again, when this happens, no nagging or scolding – even if he eventually wets his pants. If possible condition your child to urinating in different places.

Joan: And all of them as far away from the house as possible.

Doctor: Consider bringing along his own potty when you go travelling. If the little boy has not learned to stand up and urinate by the age of two, he'll catch on when he sees how his father or older boys do it. Try making a game of it. Cut some circles of bright coloured paper and float them in the toilet bowl. Then, let him play 'hit the target' with his father or brother. But even after he seems to be trained, there are going to be 'accidents' for one reason or another – stress or excitement or cold weather or a change of scene, etc.

Joan: I just hope my kid won't be accident-prone.

Doctor: And there are times when training just breaks down.

Joan: And a time when mummy just breaks down.

Doctor: I think we've become unnecessarily self-conscious and uptight about toilet training. Curiously, many women who have read or heard next to nothing about child psychology in general and toilet training in particular often manage to do a job superior to their better educated sisters, simply by using common sense and following their own sound instincts. They aren't so likely to interpret temporary resistance as hostility. They just get on with it and stick to it. So hold to the line and be of good cheer.

Joan: I'm practically dancing on air. Oh, Doctor, on my way out, would you mind terribly if I used your bathroom?

CHAPTER XIII

If You're Giving a Party for One- or Two-Year-Olds, Watch Out for Party Poopers

SEYMOUR XAVIER SCHAINHOLZ, M.D.

Dear Miss R,

Please forgive me for writing you in care of your parents but several of my bills have come back marked, "Addressee Unknown."

I recall your once telling me that your father is a doctor also. I am. sure he will be sensitive--and sympathetic--to the matter at hand and will take pains to see that this communication reaches you.

I hope all is well with you and little Melissa--or should I say, "big Melissa"?

Respectfully yours,

[signature]

P.S. I am enclosing an additional stamp to add to my return envelope as postal rates have gone up twice since I mailed it to you.

*H*ARD though it is to believe, before you know it your baby will be ready for fun, and your house will suddenly be loaded up with every kind of toy and gadget in the world.

Melissa was barely able to focus when our flat started to look like Santa's workshop. Every room was filled with bricks, dolls, choo-choo trains, mobiles and woolly animals. It was driving me crazy, as now there wasn't any room left for my bricks, dolls, choo-choo trains, mobiles and woolly animals.

I was one of those mothers who liked to give children's parties at the drop of a rattle, and by the time I realized how much bother and trouble they were, it was too late. Melissa and I were in the social swing.

From all these parties I developed a fantastic knowledge of how to entertain children which I'd like to pass on to you. I also developed an ulcer which you can have, too.

I have found that my best parties were the ones that had a theme. Some of those used which worked well were 'Balloons,' 'Sweets' and 'Tiny Toys.' But don't let the children pick the theme, or it will be 'Wreck the Joint.'

137

I always used to start the party off with organized games such as musical highchairs, pin-the-nappy-on-the-donkey and spin the bottle. When these games got the little darlings too excited, I'd give myself a break with a game of hide-and-seek. I'd tell the little darlings to hide, and I never could find them until just before refreshment time. Then to save aggravation and trouble I'd serve the cake and ice cream right on the floor.

Whatever you do, however, keep the children busy. If the party gets too relaxed, the kids may let down their hair and break toilet training – and nobody needs party poopers around.

But don't let me leave you with the wrong impression. Children's parties can be fun – especially that supremely magical moment when you hear yourself saying, 'The party's over.'

I have been saving my best advice for the last. If you really want to give your child a terrific party and save all the wear and tear on yourself, find another kid born on the same day – and persuade his mother to give the bash! Then at the end of the party, tell her she was a terrific hostess, toast her with champagne, get her smashed and take home all the expensive presents for your kid.

Doctor: Ah, but your little darling couldn't care less. Most babies prefer simple toys to the elaborate and expensive ones. The very best plaything for a one-year-old is a block that runs on wheels and has holes for pegs. Or a plain cardboard box with a string. First he'll enjoy pushing it. Then a little later he'll pull it around.

Joan: If he's all wrapped up in pushing and pulling, why can't I give him a mop?

Doctor: A baby also wants to be doing what mummy's doing. If she's cooking or putting clothes in the washing machine, then that's what the baby wants to be doing too, even if it's hard.

Joan: This mummy does something even harder than clumping around with pots and pans. She tries to knock five years off her face by putting on her eye liner, false lashes and eye shadow. Shadow, of course, is the hardest to put on as I never knew you had to shut your eyes.

Doctor: By the age of two, children become more creative. This is the time for all kinds of vehicles, dolls, doll's houses and especially bricks. A big pile of bricks is worth a bagful of other kinds of toys you could give a child in his early years. With these he is able to be a creator. One important caution for parents is not to try to hurry a child into being logical and rational in his playing.

Joan: Particularly if the father isn't logical or rational in his playing around. My husband used to date . . . oops, sorry, Doc, I was interrupting.

Doctor: A parent of a two-year-old, for example, might bring her child home a doll with a whole wardrobe for it. But when the child dresses the doll, the coat goes on first and the doll is wearing nothing underneath. Unless mummy is understanding, she might tend to get impatient.

Joan: Of course she might. The baby at this stage is supposed to be creative, and not still imitating mummy.

Doctor: Or the parent who's bought her two-year-old a model of the High Speed Train complete with tracks can get upset when the little darling takes the whole thing and throws it against the wall. But it's asking too much to expect the baby to know that the train should go right on the tracks.

Joan: Especially if his dad is off his trolley.

Doctor: Suppose someone gives the baby a box of crayons and a colouring book. He has no concept of staying within the outlined shape of objects. His crayon brushes back and forth in every direction. Nor can he be bothered with colour differentiations. Mountains and trees and deserts and houses and people may all be rendered bright purple. Just don't be peeved with him for not painting the trees green and the deserts yellow.

Joan: Peeved? I'll encourage him. If he keeps on colouring just like that he could grow up to become an Abstract Expressionist and con people into paying £50,000 for a painting.

Doctor: Just don't rush him or you'll make him feel inadequate when he can't live up to your expectations.

Joan: I know the feeling. That's how I felt the first time I went to buy a bra. The saleslady laughed and said I should come back in five years. I was twenty-four at the time and lonely. But then I never did have many friends. As a child I was so fat no one could get close enough to me to know I was fun.

Doctor: I'm sure that won't happen to your baby if you let him develop friendships early. Your little one will begin to seek out the companionship of his peers when he's one and a half or a little older. This can be an unnerving spectacle because no child of that age gives up his toys in the spirit of sharing.

Joan: I don't blame the kid. When's the last time you saw its parents sharing their stocks and shares or their jewels?

Doctor: The feeling of generosity will come to him – when he begins to have a real fondness for other children.

140

Joan: That feeling of generosity could come so gradually it might not show up till the next world. I never saw Howard Hughes or J. Paul Getty giving anything away.

Doctor: Don't force sharing on him before he's ready for it. It'll just make him clutch his possessions more firmly than ever, and he'll decide the world's a place where everybody's out to take everything away from him.

Joan: Do you really think he'll be clever enough to figure that out by the time he's two?

Doctor: When he starts getting a kick out of socializing with his young pals, you can make a little game of it: 'Okay, first it's Jimmy's turn to make anything he wants out of the bricks.'

Joan: '. . . then it's Tommy's turn to destroy it.'

Doctor: When he first starts playing with other children, your first-born may find that the other kids are grabbing his toys away from him. But very soon he'll catch on and learn how to protect his turf and get back what's his.

Joan: And everybody else's, if he's going to grow up a winner.

Doctor: If some real bully keeps giving your child a hard time, then take him somewhere else where he can find other playmates.

Joan: Whom *he* can bully.

Doctor: Sometimes it's especially hard for the first-born to learn to share, as his parents tend to fuss over him. By the time the second one comes along, most parents have learned how to relax a little more and not overdo everything.

Joan: By the time the second one comes along it's amazing that they have the energy left to even *underdo* anything.

Doctor: After a while the child should be creating his own interests and meeting the world on his own terms. But if the parents are always anticipating him, picking him up, showing him off, and getting into a stew when he's sick or badly behaved, that baby's going to believe he's the brightest star in the whole solar system. He'll expect everybody to find him charming and lovable without his making any effort to be charming and lovable. And do you know how he'll end up?

Joan: As President of the United States?

Doctor: You should also be prepared for the fact that just about the time your child is beginning to frame whole sentences, he may take special delight in rude words.

Joan: I'll be upset only if I'm told to do something with myself that's physiologically impossible. My aim is to oblige any reasonable requests.

Doctor: If you appear either shocked or amused, your youngster will know he's on to a good thing and won't let go of it. If you're really put off by rude words from small fry, the best way to cope is not to react in any way. When you've had your fill, quietly say something like, 'Those really aren't very nice things to be saying. And most people – even grown-ups – don't like to hear words like those.'

Joan: . . . in the daytime, that is.

Doctor: That's a wild thing to say, Miss Rivers.

Joan: I know, Doc, but sometimes I can't control my mouth.

Doctor: That's due to aggressiveness – which in adults or small children, particularly boys, is one of the universal facts of life. Even our movies and television are filled with it.

Joan: I've always wondered why we needed to look at violence on the screen when we can find so much of it in the home.

Doctor: As far as toys are concerned, I'm against anything more warlike than water pistols, but trying to keep a child from owning or touching any war toys is easier said than done.

Joan: Particularly when mummy keeps a loaded revolver under her pillow.

Doctor: Probably the best approach is quietly to explain your disapproval of them. Without getting preachy, you can tell him that we must all learn to be kind and friendly to one another and not go around shooting people.

Joan: Edgar and I couldn't agree more, and believe me we get this message across to all our friends by smacking it into them.

Doctor: One thing on which I wouldn't budge is refusing to let your child watch rubbish on television. I'd keep all the sadistic, savage bestiality strictly off-limits. It's definitely harmful for the small, impressionable child.

Joan: That's the perfect argument for two television sets in every home! The parents can go on slaking their thirst for violence at the same time they're teaching their kids the joys of peace.

Doctor: Another manifestation of aggression that can be a bother is the biting habit.

Joan: I know, Doc, but I can't help myself. Sometimes I get so provoked that I think the only way the baby will listen to me is if I take a good bite out of him.

Doctor: The baby who occasionally bites his playmates or his parents at this age but otherwise seems to be okay in disposition should not cause worry. If you're bitten, don't bite back or fly into a rage. At all times you must remain the benign boss. When you see those little teeth bared for action, calmly but pointedly get out of their way. He'll soon learn that it's a habit that's got to go.

Joan: Something's got to go – either the habit or his teeth.

Doctor: As far as playmates are concerned, they'll soon let

him know how much he can get away with. When you see one youngster biting or punching another, it's a mistake to rush in and try to stop him.

Joan: Sure. He might turn on me.

Doctor: Leave him alone. He'll have to take his lumps from his victim, but if mummy keeps interceding, he'll get the idea that it's okay to keep biting and slugging away as mummy will always come in time to protect him.

Joan: What if my kid turns out to be the muggee instead of the mugger?

Doctor: If your child's been on the receiving end and is really miserable or hurting, give him sympathy but don't overreact to his complaint. Look quickly for ways to distract him. Don't encourage weeping and whimpering over every little thing, but don't be afraid to be comforting. It won't make a sissy or a cry-baby out of him.

Joan: Unless he already is.

Doctor: At this age children don't differentiate between boy play and girl play. For example, no parent should be upset to see his two-year-old son playing with dolls. It is only when children get to be three or so that their sex identities sort themselves out, and boys and girls seek out activities normally associated with their gender.

Joan: Like 'Let's play Doctor and Mummy.' That would be okay, right?

Doctor: Right.

Joan: And I guess you'd only be in trouble if the little boy insisted on playing Mummy!

Doctor: Miss Rivers, if you don't mind I'd like to go back to playing doctor with my next patient.

CHAPTER XIV

Is There A Father in the House?

*A*RE daddies really necessary?

I say 'yes.' Just as every child needs a mother, it needs a daddy too. But what exactly is a daddy and who is he?

Daddy is the man who brings home the bacon – which these days costs a heck of a lot more than mother's milk.

Daddy is the thoughtful man who will suggest putting vodka in baby's bottle when he's crying.

Daddy is the guy who's quick to appear with the camera and just as quick to disappear when there's a nappy to be changed.

On the coldest of nights, he's the one who suddenly is only too happy to drive the babysitter home – once he notices that she's seventeen, nubile and has 'welcome' written on her panties. That's who daddy is.

Still, while you're providing your child with his layette, furniture and toys, also try to provide a daddy. Remember: it's a wise child who knows its own father – before the blood tests are in . . .

Doctor: Let me assure you, fathers are needed by children of both sexes.

Joan: But they never seem to be around when mummy needs them.

Doctor: Unfortunately, after a hard day at the office daddy may not always feel up to the rigours of fatherhood. However, if he knows how important his company is to the child, he should be willing to devote a reasonable amount of time to him. Quality, rather than quantity, is what is important. One index to quality is the approving attitudes of the father. Fathers sometimes expect too much – especially of sons – and they get turned off if the youngster doesn't show immediate promise of genius or athletic prowess. This gives the child the sense of not adding up to very much.

Joan: But his psychiatrist's bills will add up to plenty.

Doctor: If the father is impatient or cranky, the little boy is apt to feel out of tune with the whole world of male interests and draw closer to his mother and her interests.

Joan: Oh-oh! I'd hate to see a five-year-old boy doing bust development exercises.

Doctor: Of course, little girls need a loving daddy too.

Joan: Yes, but after 17 preferably not their own.

Doctor: A father, in appreciating and loving his little daughter, will give her confidence in herself and pleasure in being a girl.

Joan: But who wants to be a little girl these days? Everyone wants to be liberated – except me. I don't want to be liberated – I was never captured.

Doctor: Around the time children are three years old, they begin to think both their fathers and mothers are wonderful people.

Joan: A feeling destined to last ten gorgeous seconds.

Doctor: A father should share in disciplining the child. But too many fathers shy away from this job, particularly if they had fathers whose disciplining they resented. They don't want to be resented by their children, so they prefer to walk away from any unpleasantness.

Joan: Sure – let mummy do it. And let mummy get up at night. And let mummy change the dirty nappies. And let mummy clean up the messes and mend the clothes and wash the cuts and take out the splinters and what thanks does mummy get for all this? A hamburger on Mother's Day in McDonald's.

Doctor: Easy, easy, Miss Rivers. I agree with you. Fathers must help – even with the punishing. The child knows when he has punishment coming to him and when his father evades it he becomes all the more fearful. It's better for the father to clear the air. Not pleasant for the youngster, true, but he learns that he can survive it.

Joan: You know that old saying, 'Spare the rod . . . we'll need it for hanging curtains.'

Doctor: Just never forget – especially during punishing – you are a lot bigger than your child. So spank to *punish* – not to hurt. Also, the best place for a good wallop is the rear-end.

Joan: What happens if the father is never around? This would really upset a child. My friend Selma is a case in point. She had a tragic childhood. Her father died three years before she was born.

153

Doctor: There are few things we should say about absent fathers.

Joan: The most printable of which is, 'Where the hell is that bum?'

Doctor: Wherever he is, he should keep in touch.

Joan: Yes, and I guess it would be courteous to send him engagement and marriage announcements.

Doctor: He should not just be told the obvious things, like how much baby weighs or how tall he is or what his first words were, but also some of the tiny engaging details of baby's growth and development.

Joan: Such as, 'Darling, wish you could be here this very moment to see little Johnny teething on your mother's fat thighs.'

Doctor: Most importantly the father shouldn't be told that there are no problems whatsoever. That makes him feel irrelevant and not needed.

Joan: If he's gone too long, that's just what he'll be.

Doctor: On the other hand, you shouldn't burden him with decisions he can't handle from a distance or problems he can't do anything about.

Joan: Such as, 'Guess what? I'm pregnant again.'

Doctor: Now if the parents are divorced, what the mother should do is . . .

Joan: Make him pay a fortune in alimony.

Doctor: By all means, but if the father is not around, the child can still grow up without suffering psychological damage. Much depends on the mother's spirit.

Joan: It would help if she actually had a large supply of spirits.

Doctor: As best she can, she should go on with her normal routine, keeping up with her outside interests and social activities. But remember, whatever the age or sex, the child needs to be friendly with other men if the father is gone. Grandfathers, cousins, scoutmasters, old family friends . . .

Joan: . . . *young* family friends.

Doctor: All kinds of friendly men can give the child the male companionship he needs.

Joan: And even have some left over for mummy.

Doctor: If it's a boy, by the time he's two or so, he should be playing with other boys every day. Inviting lots of boys over to play at your house so your youngster can have lots of male companionship is a must.

Joan: Hey, I just thought of something. If there's no father around, the mother has to do all the disciplining . . . like getting the kid to bed on time.

Doctor: Of course, it's better when each parent can take his turn at it – but whoever does it should be cheerful but firm. Don't ask the child if he'd like to go to bed. Set a time and stick to it, but don't be so rigid that there can never be an exception. Like on Hallowe'en or Christmas Eve . . .

Joan: . . . or the night Aunt Jane's will is going to be read.

Doctor: Preparing for bed should have a little ritual about it.

Joan: Little ritual! My God, you should see what I go through. First, off come the eyelashes, the eyeshadow, the eyeliner and my wiglet. Then off comes my Cross-My-Heart bra. Then out with the

155

dentures. Then on with the creams and lotions and oils and salves. I'm so greasy, I get into bed and slide right out.

Doctor: The baby should have some hugs and kisses, be tucked in and read to a little bit, or maybe listen to a favourite record until he falls asleep. The stories shouldn't be scary or he might have a nightmare.

Joan: Well, there goes every fairy tale I know – Hansel and Gretel getting shoved in the oven, Red Riding Hood chased by the wolf, and two of the three little pigs being eaten up. The only nice fairy story I know is the love of Batman for Robin.

Doctor: How much sleep a child needs varies. But you can't assume just because he's wide awake he's getting enough sleep. There may be any number of stimulating factors that are keeping him awake. As a rule of thumb, the average two-and-a-half-year-old needs twelve hours of sleep at night and a nap of one to two hours during the day. This amount lessens gradually as he grows older.

Joan: I need a lot of sleep too. But I usually get it in little naps when I'm at the wheel on the motorway or when I'm making love.

Doctor: Another area of discipline is to get your child to perform certain tasks for himself. For example: a child starts to undress himself sometime between the ages of one and one and a half, and at about two has mastered the art. But getting his clothes on again is harder. However, let him try to do it himself and when you help him be diplomatic and don't help him too much. Again, the key word is patience. And when he does something right, be sure to praise him.

Joan: With all this talk about dressing and undressing, I've developed a chill. So may I ask you something, Doctor?

Doctor: Of course. What is it?

Joan: If we're finished for today, do you mind if I put on my clothes?

CHAPTER XV

The First Three Years Are the Hardest – Until the Fourth

*I*N the beginning there was my pregnancy, then delivery, and then nappies, formulas, colic, 2 a.m. feeds, temper tantrums, teething – and all the other joys too, too humorous to mention. But finally Melissa hit three and I saw a light at the end of the tunnel – Nursery School.

I was thrilled. At last I'd have time to myself. I thought nursery school would be good since it was really nothing more than an expensive stopgap between The Wide Awake Club and bedtime.

I turned out that I was wrong as usual. I investigated and found out there were all kinds of nursery schools. One of the best known in my area was The Fanny Hill & Dale Country Day School. It was a bit too liberal for us. Not only did they have Christmas and Easter off, they also had a holiday on Karl Marx's birthday. One mother who had pulled her Little Darling out told me they had taught arithmetic by using such problems as, 'If Johnny has five marijuana cigarettes and smokes two, how many does he have left? How many does he *think* he has left?'

The next school we investigated was more showbiz – The Raquel Welch Nursery School. The name turned me off right away as I felt they would probably place too much emphasis on the plastic arts. Also, I didn't want Melissa to go to any showbiz school. A friend of mine sent her child to one and it was terrible. When the kids auditioned for the school play, rumour had it that a 'casting crib' was involved!

We finally settled on a nice simple one: The Jack and Jill Maximum Security Nursery School. Melissa spent many happy hours there painting, playing with bricks and working in clay.

Not only did she adore it, but she also adored her twenty-year-old teacher. She kept telling me how alike we were: the same eyes, the same hairdo, the same figure. To say the least, I was extremely flattered, but I think he was a bit miffed!

I remember telling my doctor about this . . .

Doctor: It's good that your child adores her teacher and that she is happy in school. School means rules and this is good. Lots of modern theories say that all a kid needs at home is love – no rules – and that children should be allowed to give full vent to their antisocial feelings. They say that if anything goes wrong, it has to be the parents' fault . . .

Joan: . . . except if it's an earthquake. Then it's a geological fault.

Doctor: Many parents hate to discipline their children and therefore have a difficult time because they're guilt-ridden, and guilt gets in the way of handling a child easily. The child knows when he's way out of line and unconsciously wants to be stopped. If he consistently is not stopped, he will become a spoiled child. And nobody wants a spoiled child.

Joan: Because they smell bad?

Doctor: Problems often occur when parents had rough childhoods themselves. Perhaps they always had to be too 'good' for their own good and now they get some kind of inner glee in seeing their own progeny act out all the aggressions they had to keep bottled up. Kidding themselves, of course, that they're being 'modern' parents.

Joan: Remember Adam and Eve – and their delightful son, Cain! He really got away with murder.

Doctor: And he should have been stopped in childhood!

Joan: Every time I did something bad, my mother would say, 'How could you? After all the sacrifices I've made!' And she did make sacrifices for me. Once a week she would kill a chicken in front of my photograph.

Doctor: All the studies have shown that a child is happier if some standards of decently good behaviour are met.

Joan: Of course he is. But mummy and daddy may have a dickens of a time meeting them.

Doctor: If he's being rude to his parents, he should be stopped. He'll get cross with you – but let him. And also let him know that his angry feelings are quite normal. Another tip to the wise parent is, 'Tell them; don't ask them.' You hear many a mother saying, 'Shall we lunch now?' Or, 'Shall we go sit on the potty now?' This is wrong.

Joan: Of course it is. Every kid knows there isn't such a thing as a potty built for two.

Doctor: Don't give him choices. Just lead him toward the appropriate activity. For instance, if your two-year-old is pushing a toy truck around the room and you sense he should be going to the toilet, you might say, 'Now let's drive the truck on a nice long trip to the

163

toilet.' And don't get into the habit of giving him reasons why things should be done. Most of the reasons tend to have an 'or else' kind of warning. 'Don't poke Fluffy in the eye or his eye will fall out and he won't be able to see anything.' You're warning him of unhappy consequences that can fill his young head with morbid thoughts.

Joan: When otherwise it could be filling up with sordid thoughts.

Doctor: If the youngster is in danger or endangering something or somebody else, remove him. It's not necessary to give explanations for everything. At a certain age, you can get into a real hassle trying to answer the interminable 'Why?' 'Shall we go out and take a walk now?' 'Why?' 'Because we need our exercise.' 'Why?' 'Because it will help us grow strong.' 'Why?' And on into the night. So use your judgment and answer some whys but not all.

Joan: Why?

Doctor: The very small child knows he's new to the world and there's a lot he doesn't know. He depends on you to be his experienced guide.

Joan: The little fool!

Doctor: When his impulses are frustrated he may take it out on the floor or himself, pounding his hands and feet and yelling his head off, but don't be alarmed. A temper tantrum once in a while doesn't mean too much. If you see it coming, the best thing is to head it off with some pleasant distraction.

Joan: But you just can't just start breast-feeding him any old time and place. I know. I'll give him a rattle – with the snake still on the end of it.

164

Doctor: When the storm does break, keep out of the baby's way and take it easy until the thing subsides. There's no sense to a tantrum if there's no audience.

Joan: Good, I'll go on that long-deferred trip to Bermuda.

Doctor: Whatever you do, don't give in to his demand or he'll be throwing a tantrum every time there's a tug of wills.

Joan: Could it be a time to give him something to really yammer about? Like a smack on the bottom?

Doctor: No, when a child is in the middle of a tantrum, it's no time to be angry with him or try to reason with him. The best thing is to try to find him some face-saving out. You can quietly disappear and hope the storm will soon blow over. Or if the baby's headstrong and he seems hell-bent on yelling you into an institution, after a while you might pop in with some friendly make-up overture. A hug and kiss and maybe a suggestion for something fun to do.

Joan: Such as, 'Come on, Dickie, let's see who can hold his head longer under the bath water.'

Doctor: Where your mettle will really be tested is when your child throws a temper tantrum in some very public place. If you can manage it, pick him up with a cheery expression and hurry into some quiet corner where your passions can cool.

Joan: Such as my car. That way the kid can scream all he wants to and get away with murder, and I can laugh all I want to and get away with thirty-two pounds worth of free groceries.

Doctor: And don't be thrown by the breath-holding bit.

Joan: Thrown! I'm delighted when a kid holds his breath – especially if he's just eaten garlic or smoked a cigar.

165

FATHER KNOWS BEST – WHICH IS WHY MOTHERS HAVE THE BABY.

Doctor: When a child holds his breath during a tantrum, ignore it and keep your cool. Remember, he will stop holding his breath.

Joan: The moment he loses consciousness.

Doctor: Talking about tempers brings us to the subject of punishment. To punish or not to punish.

Joan: Is *not* the question when a kid deserves it.

Doctor: Yes, it is. Some parents' discipline seems to be firm enough to hold up without resorting to punishment.

Joan: I've always felt it isn't hard to rear a child as long as it has a rear.

Doctor: The thing to remember is that punishment is never the vital element in training a child. It's being loved and learning to love back. When a child starts to think his parents are wonderful and he wants to imitate them, he does a lot to civilize himself. But he needs direction. In football parlance, he's the player but you're the coach.

Joan: I hate to think of my kid growing up to be a football player. They're so stupid. I was with one in a lift once. The operator called out the floors and he tackled her.

Doctor: Day by day, it's the job of the parent to keep the child in training with love and strength and a reasonable show of predictability. If the system breaks down and too many rules get broken, the time may be at hand for severer measures.

Joan: Then it's twenty laps around the track and no wine, women or song for a week.

Doctor: There's a reaction in recent times against spanking. But if it's a choice of spanking or prolonged nagging or trying to make a child feel unduly guilty, I'll take the spanking.

Joan: Easy for you to say. Who'd dare to spank a doctor?

Doctor: Some authorities recommend that if you're going to spank, never do it in anger. Of course, sometimes the go-to-your-room ploy works. But the danger there is the child might begin to think of his room as a prison.

Joan: I'd have to do a lot of redecorating to make it look that good.

Doctor: Other parents make the naughty child sit off by himself in a special chair, but the thing I don't like at all is threats, especially the kind that are totally ridiculous and can't be followed through on. For example: 'If you don't go to sleep this instant, the big bad wolf is going to come and get you.' Also, parents who always have to resort to punishment obviously have a problem, and the problem is themselves. In some way they are inviting bad behaviour from their children and then they act surprised when it comes. These people need help.

Joan: Who doesn't! But where do you find good help these days?

Doctor: Most parents want their children to have good manners, but it's hard to force them on a child. He'll learn them when he's learned to like other people. First, you have to make him feel easy with strangers.

Joan: How can I when I've already told him never to speak to one?

SEYMOUR XAVIER SCHAINHOLZ, M.D.

Dear Miss Rivers:

It was a pleasure to finally get through to you on the phone the other day and I could hardly believe that it was Melissa who answered it.

At your suggestion I am resubmitting my statement. I can well appreciate your confession that you threw out the last one thinking it was "junk mail."

Naturally I hope I have better luck this time around.

Most sincerely,

Doctor:	I mean, people that are strangers to him. Your friends.
Joan:	Who are pretty strange, come to think of it.
Doctor:	The thing is don't introduce him right off to a new grown-up and expect him to respond with the usual niceties. This embarrasses him.
Joan:	But think how it embarrasses mummy to have my kid stand there with his eyes cast down, struck dumb and rolling his head around like a yo-yo. My friends will think he's a cheeky kid who is imitating them.
Doctor:	For approximately the first three years, a child needs time to size up a stranger. While he does this, it's best to steer the conversation away from him, rather than making him the subject under discussion. When he sees you talking casually to a new person for a few minutes, he might feel comfortable enough to break into the conversation.
Joan:	With some choice announcement like, 'Mummy, Spot's on heat again.'
Doctor:	Admittedly his conversational gambits might not be for high society. But if a child's feeling of friendliness towards others keeps growing, it'll be reflected in more acceptable conversation.
Joan:	Which means all he'll ever discuss is having sex and tax havens . . . or is it having sex in tax havens.
Doctor:	The best way for a child to learn to be kind and polite is to watch his own family.
Joan:	In that case, my kid may have to look for foster parents. My husband is so rude to me! The other day I said to him, 'Nothing I do pleases you any more. I'm going home to Mother.' He said, '*That* pleases me.'

Doctor: A child does have to learn to say 'please' and 'thank you' and 'I'm sorry' when dealing with people. But teach your baby gently. And do it in private to save him embarrassment.

Joan: You mean wait until you get home before you tell Johnny he shouldn't have asked nice Mrs Johnson next door why she has a moustache?

Doctor: Yes. Unless Mrs Johnson happens to be proud of her moustache and purposely cultivated it.

Joan: To go with her mink coat, no doubt.

Doctor: You'll find between the ages of two and three, the child goes through a stubborn contrary phase. He thinks he is being bossed too much, but is bossy himself. He wants to do everything his own way. He can't make up his mind and once he does, he immediately wants to change it. But cheer up. There are better days coming.

Joan: If you believe in the hereafter.

Doctor: To a degree let him have his head. Allow a little more time for getting things done. Let him do as much as he can for himself. Steer him gently toward the 'must-do' things with a pleasant flow of chatter. Sometimes you see a dawdling child with a mother who prods him from morning to night.

Joan: Now let me join in with the refrain: 'He wasn't born that way. It's his mother's doing.'

Doctor: You've guessed the villain. The mother. That nervous, nagging mother who's always anticipating that he won't do what he should. All this pressure on the child naturally sets up the contrariness that makes the prodding seem necessary. The wise thing is to give him a reasonable chance to do what he

170

should be doing. If that doesn't work, remind him gently to shape up, but remember small children love to do things that get them dirty, like mucking around in the dirt and smearing themselves with mud. It makes them feel good.

Joan: Just as it makes mummy feel good. I once spent £25 for a full mud pack and I never looked better. Then about the third day, the mud fell off.

Doctor: It's unhealthy to limit such activities for they are natural and necessary. If he's thwarted, it'll make him hold back in other ways and he may not grow into the warm, spontaneous life-embracing little person you hope he's going to be.

Joan: When does that warm, spontaneous life-embracing little person get out from underfoot and start making it on his own?

Doctor: Three is none too early to start your child at playgroup or nursery school if he is in an area without any other children. In fact it's highly desirable. Some mothers say, 'Oh, I think I'll wait another year. Little Janie will get so much more out of it when she's four.' This misses the point of playgroups or nursery schools. The value is not so much in what they get out of classes or activities, but in the children's joy in one another's companionship.

Joan: And there's the joy mummy gets in sharing her little treasure with others, since the sharing takes place away from her. On days off from school, I find that sandpits are great substitutes for baby sitters. I know of several silly kids who just sit in them for hours waiting for the tide to come in.

Doctor: Whether it's playing in a sandpit or backyard mud, just don't make your child feel he is doing something really messy or disgusting.

Joan: Like engaging in sex play?

Doctor: You'll have to contend with that too at about this time.

Joan: I'd love to contend with it if I didn't already have the kid to contend with.

Doctor: We know that interest in sex begins practically at birth. But even so, parents find it upsetting to see young children engaged in sex play with themselves or others.

Joan: Can you wonder? You want the best for your kids and all that. But who wants to see a three-year-old already making out better than you are?

Doctor: Around the age of three, there's natural curiosity about why little boys are made differently from little girls. Unless this curiosity is satisfied, youngsters may go on harbouring fears about themselves. Little David sees that his baby sister doesn't have a penis and he wonders if something happened to it. Then you explain that there are two kinds of people. He's like his father and Uncle Harry and Cousin Joe, and his baby sister is like Mummy and Grandma and Aunt Helen.

Joan: And Uncle Charlie – after his trip to Denmark. Charlie had a change-of-sex operation and now I'm so confused as to what he is, that for his birthday I gave him a set of his and hers towels.

Doctor: Little girls need to be cheerfully assured, too, that nothing has happened to them – that they never had a penis and it's just fine to be the way they are.

Joan: It must be. Look who gets all the obscene phone calls.

Doctor: Also, remember the handling of the genitals begins very early. Around the age of three it may be related to the fears we were just discussing. This is a time when children's feelings are very intense. In any event, you discourage it – as you do sex play between

youngsters – but don't act shocked or outraged or
disgusted.

Joan: The way I did on my wedding night?

Doctor: With or without your help a child's sex education
keeps expanding. But he'll be better off if he can go
to you with his questions.

Joan: That way, he'll be kept in the dark that much longer.

Doctor: The conscientious mother can sometimes go into
more detail with explanations than the child wants or
can absorb. A three-year-old will probably be asking
where babies come from. The best answer to that is:
'From a seed that grows inside mummy.' That's all.
One thing I'd advise against is blaming babies on the
stork.

Joan: Too right! I never heard of anyone making love to a
stork! I'll just tell him what my mother told me. The
recipe for having a baby is simply to take one man
and one woman and mix well.

Doctor: Much of this education will come gradually through
contact with their peers. In playgroup or nursery
school they will probably get the chance to take care
of pets. This is extremely educational.

Joan: Especially monkeys. To this day I run to the zoo
every Sunday to watch. A friend of mine used to
squint and pretend it was a guy and a girl doing it in
fur coats.

Doctor: Children of three, as we've said, have a pretty clear
idea of their sex identities. It's really a wonderful
time in the parents' lives. The children idolize them.
Boys want to be like their fathers and girls want to be
like their mothers. Little boys and girls develop
romantic feelings about the parents of the opposite

sex. Young David is likely to say to his mother, 'Mummy, I want to marry you.'

Joan: Mummy could do a lot worse – and probably already has.

Doctor: The wise parent thanks her child for the compliment but tactfully explains that she already is married, and that the child will grow up and pick out his own wife.

Joan: You know what, Doc?

Doctor: What?

Joan: After our many little talks, I've come to the conclusion that in spite of all the work and mess and bother involved, there's nothing like having a child. Why, I'd rather have my darling baby than a million pounds.

Doctor: Really?

Joan: Absolutely! Because when you have a million pounds you want another million, but when you have a kid . . .

CHAPTER XVI

You'll Still Be Seeing Your Gynaecologist . . . and He'll Be Seeing Everything!

OKAY, you've had your baby. The kid is doing find and you're a fulfilled woman at last. So what do you do now?

As a mature, informed woman you know you should go to the gynaecologist for check-ups every six months, right? But no woman likes to go to the gynaecologist. And without the shield of your tummy in front of you, you suddenly feel *very* aware of the situation and how much you dread these embarrassing visits.

First of all, he never gets to see the pretty underwear that you put on just for him – thanks to his nasty nurse, who is obviously in love with him and understandably resents your superior looks. She's not going to let you flaunt any seductive dainties before his eyes. So she puts you in that little room and makes you take off everything. And I mean *everything*. (I had one nurse once who made me take off a corn plaster.) Then she puts you in that lumpish whiteish gown with the slit up the back and hands you a huge bottle.

'Here,' she says haughtily. 'The doctor will want a sample of your urine.'

This always hurts me. After all these years, either he wants it or he doesn't. I'm tired of giving free samples!

After the sample bit is over, the nurse puts you on that table with the paper covering and puts your feet in the stirrups. 'Move down, move down,' she keeps saying. I don't know about you, but I *can't* move. I'm stuck to the paper. Then she covers you up with that sheet that covers up nothing and tells you to relax. 'Doctor will be right in.'

There you are alone . . . for eternities. Facing you *revoltingly* is that cabinet filled with those shiny, enormous instruments that could not possibly fit inside a mother of fourteen, much less little me.

Finally . . . the good doctor makes his entrance. He takes one glance at your immaculate body which is fresh out of a three-hour bath *and* he has the nerve and tactlessness to don a pair of rubber gloves!

Somehow, I always find myself in the hands of doctors who think they are comedians. I want to say to them, 'You stick to your scalpeling and leave the jokes to me.' Because I don't think doctors should be funny. What ails us is not a laughing matter.

I had a friend, if I may digress a moment, who underwent major surgery. When he came out of his anaesthetic, the doctor was by his bed chuckling to himself.

'Mr X,' said the doctor (a shortened version of my friend's original name, which was Xsky), 'I have both good news and bad news for you.'

'Give me the bad news first,' whispered Mr X.

'Well, we had to remove both your legs.'

'What's the good news?'

'We sold your slippers,' said the doctor, cracking up.

In a gynaecologist, the last thing you're looking for is fun and games. You're distraught and humiliated enough at the absurd position you're in without having the doctor, while he's examining you, go, 'Coochie coochie coo.'

Part II in the gynaecological exam is equally off-putting. You sit with the doctor in his modern, plant-filled office and the conversation takes such an indelicate turn. It may be just my

182

repressed upbringing but somehow I hardly think 'discharges' is a fit subject to be discussing with a mature, attractive man, unless you're talking about soldiers getting out of the army.

What also drives me crazy is having to get the prescription the doctor gives you. The cost of the pills he prescribes is exorbitant. I get around this monthly drain by taking a pill every *other* day. My gynaecologist found out about this and said I was playing a dangerous game – 'Baby Roulette.'

So what's the solution? We really should go to the gynaecologist every six months and be examined. My best advice is to find a good one and to keep the relationship on a strictly professional basis. In other words, someone outside your social circle and whom you're unlikely to meet in a social situation.

I'll never forget the time I went to a dinner party and drew for my dinner partner my very own gynaecologist. 'Hello, Joan,' he smiled. As I had all my clothes on and my face was almost totally camouflaged under my heavy evening makeup, I couldn't understand how he recognized me. 'Hey, Doc,' I blurted out, 'how'd you know it was me?' 'Easy,' said my doctor, grinning, 'when you dropped your fork.'

SEYMOUR XAVIER SCHAINHOLZ, M.D.

Miss Rivers:

I was most upset when the check you claimed was "in the mail" never arrived.

Your prompt payment of my bill would be so much appreciated, needless to say, at this particular time.

Sincerely,

*H*ELLO, Doctor, I'm sorry to disturb you on a Tuesday as I know this is your morning to make out your inflated accounts for your private patients but I just had to talk to you . . . Yes, I'll be brief . . . You see, my darling baby is three now and off to nursery school and so clever that when my husband and I discuss anything in front of her, we have to purposely misspell words. Plus the child is gorgeous. She has my eyes, my nose, my mouth, my hair. The only thing that worries me a bit is one day I might need them back . . . I *am* getting to the point, Doc . . . You see, I have never looked or felt better, if I do say so myself. But I don't have to. Why only the other day, our garage mechanic said, 'That's some chassis you've got there,' and he wasn't looking at my car. The stretch marks are practically all gone and with lots of workouts at my gym I've got my old figure back or what's even better, I haven't got my old figure back, but a new and firmer one. And I've bought a new wardrobe of six divine tracksuits so I won't have to shave my legs all winter and next month my darling daughter and I will sit for our portrait. We have such a close relationship. We're almost like mother and daughter . . . Wait, Doc, hold on . . . just two minutes

187

more . . . My husband has never adored me more than now that I've fulfilled my role as M*O*T*H*E*R. Why, he's put me on a pedestal and, even though I have to dust it, it's worth it. But you see, finally, after four difficult years, I have the time to dust if I want to and decorate my home and go out to mad lunches with girl friends. Stop rushing me, Doc, I am getting to the point and just remember, I knew you before abortions were legalized. In those days, you were glad to get a call . . . Anyhow, now that I'm a Ma, I've decided to go back to university and get my M.A. I read philosophy, you know. What good did philosophy do me these last couple of years with a screaming, wet kid on my hands? All I could use it for was to prove to myself that the dirty nappies didn't really exist. Oh, and the joy of joys, I'm back to reading again. Serious reading, I mean. Not Spock. Spillane . . . Okay, okay, I know you're not interested in all this garbage . . . So, why am I calling you if everything is so terrific? Well, you see, Doc, up until this morning I really was the happiest and fittest of women. But I woke up feeling perfectly horrible. Headache. Heartburn. Nausea. I felt absolutely bushed. And I blush to bring up such intimate symptoms, especially as I know your receptionist is listening in, but my you-know-what is long, long overdue and . . .

HIGH CLASS COLLECTION AGENCY

Dear Ms. Robers,

Our client, Seemore X. Shainholz, gave us his bill for collection.

It would be a pity if a nice goil like you were to come out of a club one night and find herself in the presence of our enforcers. They are not a good audience. Pay up or we will repossess.

Hy Klass

188

SECOND LETTER FROM A REAL DOCTOR—

Dearest ~~Daughter, Joanie, Jean~~, Ms. Rivers,

I have in front of me your request for approval of your manuscript, <u>Having a Baby Can Be a Scream</u>. First of all, let me state that signing the request, "Your adoring daughter, Joan," is the kind of begging behavior which your mother and I tried to break you of many years ago. Your dog learned to have a sense of dignity. I don't know why you didn't.

Putting aside your special pleading and dealing with the manuscript itself, I can only say that conveying sound medical and psychological advice in terms comprehensible to the average person is strictly against all known and approved medical procedures, and I certainly cannot be a party to it. Next thing you know, they will be asking us to write our prescriptions legibly.

Anyhow, getting back to your manuscript, all the advice you have in there is very sound and correct. Lord knows, it is what your mother and I used in raising you. On second thought, maybe it is not such good advice.

Nothing else is new, except the pond's frozen over, but in spite of this we had a bumper crop of rutabagas this year, which surprised everyone as we live in the heart of New York City.

Please keep in touch--but not too closely. A large check in the mail each month is the best way as it serves to tell us that your memory is functioning and that you are doing well.

Your loving father,

Meyer L. Rivers, M.D.

P.S. Mother thought that this might be a good opportunity to tell you that you're not ours. We were originally going to write you a separate letter--but why waste postage?

190